PRAISE FOR *LEADING PROCUREMENT STRATEGY*

D0165069

'Great to see a relevant and rich set of practical tools, several of which, including the sourcing gemstone, we use in our organization. This book can help equip the talent of the future for the growing business value that procurement can drive and achieve.'
Michael DeWitt, Vice President, Strategic Sourcing, Walmart International

'The future of procurement is promising and exciting. Procurement will continue to innovate, become more digitized and grow its contributions to sustainability. This book will help equip more leaders of the future to help make progress happen.'
Ninian Wilson, Group Procurement Director, Vodafone

'Provides insight on the role of procurement and how it is critical for any organization's performance enhancement. The authors share great content about how procurement decisions directly impact the business community as well as creating competitive advantage for the organization.'
Lindle Hatton, CEO, National Association of State Procurement Officials (NASPO)

'Powerfully insightful and a rich source of information that demystifies the complexities of today's global supply chains. With sage, actionable thoughts, it is an essential companion in transforming procurement leadership strategy, which is certainly an integral element of creating value in the NGO sector.'
Mark Spencer, Director of Procurement and Supply Chain, Mercy Corps

'Procurement will make a huge difference to the future of our planet if we live up to our responsibility. We therefore need more people to join the effort and this book shows the opportunity and provides you with practical approaches to get there.'

Thomas Udesen, Chief Procurement Officer, Bayer and Co-founder of The Sustainable Procurement Pledge

Leading Procurement Strategy

Driving value through the supply chain

THIRD EDITION

Carlos Mena

Remko van Hoek

Martin Christopher

KoganPage

First published in Great Britain and the United States in 2014 by Kogan Page Limited
Third edition published in 2021

2nd Floor, 45 Gee Street	122 W 27th St, 10th Floor	4737/23 Ansari Road
London	New York, NY 10001	Daryaganj
EC1V 3RS	USA	New Delhi 110002
United Kingdom		India

www.koganpage.com

Kogan Page books are printed on paper from sustainable forests.

© Carlos Mena, Remko van Hoek and Martin Christopher, 2014, 2018, 2021

The rights of Carlos Mena, Remko van Hoek and Martin Christopher to be identified as the authors of this work have been asserted by them in accordance with the Copyright, Designs and Patents Act 1988.

ISBNs

Hardback	978 1 3986 0160 4
Paperback	978 1 3986 0158 1
Ebook	978 1 3986 0159 8

British Library Cataloguing-in-Publication Data

A CIP record for this book is available from the British Library.

Library of Congress Cataloging-in-Publication Data

Names: Mena, Carlos,1972- author. | Hoek, Remko |.
Van, author.|
    Christopher, Martin, author.
Title: Leading procurement strategy: driving value
through the supply
    chain / Carlos Mena, Remko van Hoek, Martin
Christoper.
Description: Third edition. | London ; New York :
KoganPage, 2021. |
    Includes bibliographical references and index.
Identifiers: LCCN 2021023595 (print) | LCCN 2021023596
(ebook) | ISBN
    9781398601604 (hardback) | ISBN 9781398601581
(paperback) | ISBN
    9781398601598 (ebook)
Subjects: LCSH: Industrial procurement.
Classification: LCC HD39.5 .M447 2021 (print) | LCC
HD39.5 (ebook) | DDC

Typeset by Integra Software Services, Pondicherry
Print production managed by Jellyfish
Printed and bound by CPI Group (UK) Ltd, Croydon, CR0 4YY

*To Lupita, Karen, Sandra, Maryl,
Ticho, Dylan, Jason and Margaret*

CONTENTS

PART TWO
Procurement and the supply network

PART THREE
Delivering performance in procurement

07 The impact of procurement on financial results 125
Simon Templar

08 Supply chain risk management 157
Martin Christopher

09 Digitization of procurement: The enabling role of technology 179
Remko van Hoek

ABOUT THE AUTHORS

Dr Carlos Mena is the Nike Professor of Supply Chain Management at Portland State University (PSU). Prior to joining PSU he was a faculty member at Michigan State University and at Cranfield University (UK). The focus of his research is the impact of procurement and supply chain management practices on economic, social and environmental performance.

Dr Remko van Hoek is Professor at the Supply Chain Management Department of the University of Arkansas, Sam M Walton College of Business. He is also an independent advisor to several companies on sourcing and procurement. Previously he was Chief Procurement Officer at the Walt Disney Company and he held procurement and supply chain executive roles in both the United States and Europe at several companies, including Nike, Cofely (GDF SUEZ) and PwC.

Dr Martin Christopher has been at the forefront of the development of new thinking in supply chain management for over 30 years. His contribution to the theory and practice of supply chain management is reflected in the many international awards that he has received. His published work is widely cited by other scholars and he has been invited to participate in academic and industry events around the world. He is an Emeritus Professor at Cranfield School of Management, UK.

Guest authors

Dr Lisa M Ellram is the Rees Distinguished Professor of Supply Chain Management in the Department of Management at the Farmer School of Business, Miami University in Oxford, OH, where she teaches logistics and supply chain management at the undergraduate and graduate level. Prior to that, she was the John Bebbling Professor of Supply Management at Arizona State University's W P Carey School of Business. She has co-authored over 100 articles and six books, the most recent being *Logistics Management: Enhancing competitiveness and customer value*. She has served as the Director for the ATK Center for Strategic Supply Leadership, and has been a member of the CAPS Research board of directors. She has taught in over 20 countries across the globe. She currently serves as a senior editor for the *Journal of Purchasing and Supply Management*, and is also on the advisory board of a number of top academic journals.

Dr Simon Templar is management accountant with over 20 years' experience in industry, ranging from 'bananas to telecommunications' in a wide range of management roles, before joining Cranfield University. He completed his PhD at Cranfield in 2013, which explored the impact of transfer pricing on supply chain management decisions. Simon is a founding member of the Supply Chain Finance Community, a not-for-profit association, which aims to share SCF good practice and new research in an open, collaborative environment. He co-authored *Financing the End-To-End Supply Chain: A reference guide to supply chain finance*. He is a visiting fellow at Cranfield University, lecturing on MSc programmes including Logistics and Supply Chain Management, Strategic Marketing and Management.

FOREWORD

It is over 35 years ago that I first ran into procurement as a source of strategic value and relevance for the company. Writing the first *Harvard Business Review* article about procurement in 1983 led to the introduction of what became the most commonly used supplier segmentation in procurement. Since then a lot has happened and I am now convinced more than ever that procurement is critical for enterprise performance enhancement. Procurement and supplier-facing activities are fundamentally commercial in nature and as a result need top talent. In fact, procurement may be too small a word for what the function does and supply chain is a better reference. Procurement executives and managers can be proud of how much has been achieved. Most companies now have a chief procurement officer reporting to the board and procurement teams are impacting performance across the business. The impact spans not only cost competitiveness but also sustainability, innovation, risk and cash management to name just a few. As a result students of procurement can be excited about what is to come and how much is still to be done. Procurement is becoming a very good part of the organization for those seeking to make a mark, have demonstrable ROI and exposure to many parts of the business and commercial processes.

It is with pleasure that I learn about this book focused on developing leaders of the future and turning thought leadership into action. Precisely what we need for the next 35 years!

Peter Kraljic
Director Emeritus, McKinsey & Company

PART ONE

Procurement strategy

01

Introduction

The strategic role of procurement

The most strategic decisions in an organization are made around the boardroom table; however, the procurement function is often conspicuous by its absence. In many organizations, the chief procurement officer (CPO) or purchasing director reports to another function such as finance, operations or supply chain and does not have a seat at the table.

While some organizations have recognized the strategic value of procurement, many have yet to realize the potential benefits it offers in terms of quality, innovation, sustainability and, most notably, resilience. The COVID-19 pandemic has shown the devastating impact that systemic risks can cause on supply chains. Across product categories, from ventilators to vaccines, it has become evident that procurement decisions directly impact business continuity. As sad as it is, this realization should serve as the catalyst that makes procurement a more strategic and influential business function.

In this chapter, we first explore how procurement can create competitive advantage for any organization, discussing its potential contribution to both the top and bottom line. We then evaluate how to maximize the impact of procurement by developing and delivering strategies, aligned internally with the needs of the organization, and externally with the requirements of customers and suppliers. Finally, we look at the leadership role that procurement can play, not only within its organization but also across the entire supply base. In essence, in this chapter we argue why procurement deserves a seat at the boardroom table and how we can present this argument.

Procurement and its impact on the bottom line

The impact of procurement decisions on the bottom line has long been recognized. On average organizations spend around 40 per cent of their sales revenue on external goods and services (CAPS, 2017). For some, this figure can be much higher, for instance, a retailer such as Walmart spends around 75 per cent of its revenues in sourcing the products it sells to consumers. This means that every $1 saved in purchasing is equivalent to about $4 in additional sales.

Figure 1.1 presents a cross-industry comparison of the proportion of spend in relation to sales. It shows that sectors such as industrial manufacturing and aerospace and defence spend around 45 per cent

FIGURE 1.1 Spend as a percentage of sales: cross-industry comparison 2017

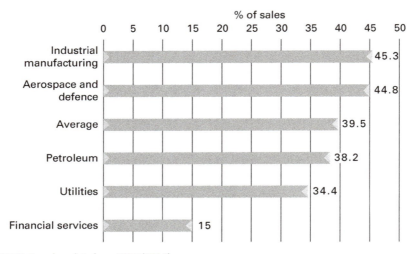

SOURCE Based on data from CAPS (2017)

of their revenues on raw materials and services, giving procurement a big responsibility. For other sectors, like financial services, this proportion is considerably lower.

Procurement and sustainable competitive advantage

Given the substantial impact that sourcing products and services has on the bottom line, procurement professionals are often proud of negotiating great deals and achieving cost reductions. However, a myopic focus on 'deals' can be a distraction from a more strategic role of procurement – its impact on long-term competitive advantage. Failing to recognize that procurement is the gateway to the supply base, which can bring innovation, quality, technology and access to new markets, would be a significant oversight.

Organizations gain competitive advantage through the use of resources at their disposal. These resources allow organizations to exploit opportunities or neutralize threats, leading to superior long-term performance (Barney, 1991, 1995). These can include scarce physical resources (eg land or raw materials), human resources, know-how, technological resources, financial resources and intangible resources (eg reputation).

Traditionally, organizations have sought to develop and exploit internal resources to create competitive advantage. However, managers increasingly recognize that they can tap into resources beyond their own four walls, by establishing appropriate external relationships, finding synergies and creating new complementary resources (Dyer and Singh, 1998; Lavie, 2006). This opens the doors for procurement to play a strategic role in developing and sustaining competitive advantage.

Figure 1.2 depicts how both 1) organizational (internal) and 2) supply base (external) resources can lead to 3) short-term competitive advantage. For these resources to contribute to competitive advantage they need to be valuable (ie they can make the organization more efficient and effective), rare (ie they are not possessed by large numbers of organizations) and appropriable (ie once an

FIGURE 1.2   Procurement and sustainable competitive advantage

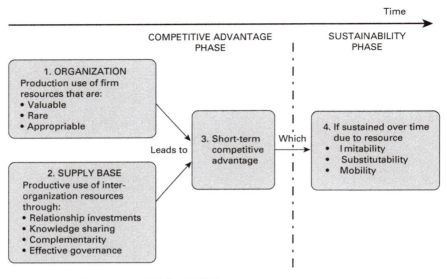

SOURCE Adapted from Wade and Hulland (2004)

organization appropriates them, they cannot be exploited by others). Eventually, some of these resources that are difficult to imitate or substitute can lead to 4) *sustainable* competitive advantage.

The procurement function contributes to organizational resources mainly through knowledge of the supply market (eg commodities buying, contracting) and skills (eg global sourcing, negotiation, specification development). These resources are extremely valuable to an organization, and sometimes can be rare. For instance, the scarcity of procurement talent can become a source of competitive advantage for organizations that manage to attract, develop and retain the best procurement professionals. However, procurement's most significant contribution to competitive advantage is through the supply network's external sources (see Tesla's supplier innovation case study).

CASE STUDY
Supplier innovation at Tesla, Inc

The automotive industry is undergoing its most significant revolution in a hundred years. The combination of electrification, autonomous vehicles technologies and changing mobility trends, such as ridesharing, are altering the competitive landscape, and new players are challenging established companies. Arguably, the most recognizable of these new players is Tesla.

Tesla was established in 2003 by a group of engineers who aspired to prove that electric vehicles could be fast and pleasurable to drive. In 2008 they introduced an all-electric sedan called Model S, capable of accelerating from 0–60 mph in 2.28 seconds. In 2015 they unveiled an SUV – Model X – and in 2017 they started delivering a low-price, high-volume vehicle called Model 3. Three years later, they launched Model Y, a compact crossover utility vehicle based on the same platform as the Model 3. These new models have dramatically boosted sales. In 2020 alone the company sold almost 500,000 vehicles and has now produced over 1 million units.

Central to Tesla's success has been its iconic CEO, Elon Musk. Musk is well known for setting very ambitious targets and sometimes criticized for not delivering, at least, not on time. However, his ambition and determination have played a role in inspiring employees and suppliers alike. One of their suppliers noted: 'Tesla is extremely aggressive, but takes a position that they are the innovator and will drive technology to the supply base' (Toolan, 2016).

Tesla's supply chain approach has been unorthodox. First, they bought an old assembly plant from NUMMI – a joint venture between General Motors and Toyota – in Fremont, California. Then, they decided to maintain tight control over a range of components by building them in-house, bucking outsourcing trends in the industry. When they source externally, they seek short-term, single-source agreements, to allow them more flexibility. However, they also recognize that innovation requires relationships with key partners that have the right expertise. Such a partnership has been established with Panasonic, the sole supplier of batteries for all their models.

Together with Panasonic, they built Gigafactory 1 in 2017, an enormous lithiumion battery factory in Nevada, which will cut battery costs by at least 30 per cent. More recently, they have again joined forces with Panasonic to build Gigafactory 2, a new facility making solar cells in Buffalo, NY.

A recent survey by Deloitte shows that suppliers prefer to build relationships with customers that encourage innovation. More than half of the suppliers responding indicated that they would withhold their most innovative products from automakers that do not participate in collaborative relationships. This approach gives Tesla an edge over its competitors who are perceived to be more conservative and slower to respond.

SOURCES Hogg (2016); Tesla (2014, 2020); Toolan (2016); Wernle (2015)

Procurement can stimulate the development of network resources in four different ways (Dyer and Singh, 1998):

1 *Investing in relationship*: Procurement can work together with suppliers to invest in relationship-specific assets, such as new facilities or equipment, leading to competitive advantage. This collaboration is usually achieved by providing safeguards and volume commitments that give suppliers the confidence to invest in those assets.

2 *Sharing knowledge*: The ability to innovate through co-creation of products and services with suppliers is increasingly recognized as a key to competitiveness. However, this requires a high degree of knowledge sharing and the ability to learn from other organizations. By investing in knowledge-sharing activities, aligning incentives to encourage transparency and reciprocity, and discouraging free-riding, organizations can tap into this innovation potential.

3 *Finding complementarity*: Organizations can also create competitive advantage with their suppliers by leveraging complementary resources with suppliers. Complementarity means that two or more organizations can achieve something together that they could not accomplish independently. This requires the procurement function to identify suppliers with potentially complementary resources (through supplier selection) and put in place the necessary mechanisms to access the benefits from complementary strategic resources, by aligning systems, processes and cultures (supplier development and relationship management).

4 *Establishing effective governance*: This is the ability to choose governance structures that reduce transaction costs and mitigate supply chain risks. It can be achieved either through contracts or self-enforcing agreements that rely on trust and goodwill. The key

is to align relationships and specific transactions with governance structures.

An important consideration in supply chain governance structures is how to protect the organization from risks in the supply base. Global supply chains are vulnerable to events such as natural disasters; intellectual property rights (IPR) infringements; ethical violations; and other forms of opportunism from suppliers. Lacking the right governance structures to manage these risks can have a strong impact on an organization's reputation and performance.

To develop a sustainable competitive advantage, organizations not only need to identify and tap into resources in the supply chain but also to do it in a way that is difficult for competitors to imitate.

The changing role of procurement

Procurement has gradually transformed from a clerical activity into a strategic function. In the 1980s there were strong calls for moving from the routine of transactional purchasing to supply management, where companies have a thorough understanding of internal requirements and the supply market, and can establish their strategic positioning for different kinds of supplies (Kraljic, 1983).

In the 1990s, with outsourcing and global sourcing trends on the rise, there were increasing calls for procurement to become a more prominent and strategic function in organizations. However, a study by Cammish and Keough (1991) revealed that in many cases, the procurement function lacked seniority and had limited access to top management. Furthermore, they found that procurement managers were paid less than their counterparts in other functions and were perceived to have little impact on performance. To change this situation, the advice was to move towards greater cross-unit coordination and more central control of the purchasing activities, to reduce total system cost rather than just unit cost.

At the turn of the 21st century, the effects of longer, more fragmented and more complex supply chains started to increase risk exposure for organizations. Events such as natural disasters, acts of terrorism, political instability and global pandemics showed that, in an increasingly globalized and interconnected world, procurement decisions have to take into account risk and vulnerabilities across the entire chain.

Another significant trend during the 'noughties' was the emergence of sustainability and corporate social responsibility. Greenhouse gas emissions, waste, pollution, scarcity of natural resources, workers' rights and child labour are among a long list of sustainability-related issues that affect procurement. Both the increasing risk in supply chains and the greater importance of sustainability call for a change in the role of and a new set of skills from procurement professionals.

The 2010s started amid a deep economic recession following a global financial crisis in 2007–8. In some respects, this situation was detrimental to the development of procurement as a strategic function because many firms had reverted to an obsessive focus on cost, at the expense of other critical factors such as value, sustainability and resilience. Procurement can have a significant short-term impact on cost by putting pressure on suppliers to reduce prices. Still, this impact is often short-lived and can damage relationships with trustworthy suppliers that might be needed in times of trouble. Ten years later, the COVID-19 pandemic has exposed how procurement and supply chain decisions can expose (and protect) organizations from risks. This realization is likely to broaden the focus and reach of procurement, as organizations seek to create more agile and resilient supply chains.

While the role of procurement has changed over time and generally has become more strategic, some organizations and even entire industries have been left behind. Maturity models, such as the one depicted in Table 1.1, represent the different stages of development of the procurement function. The maturity model presents four stages in the development of the procurement function:

1 *Transactional procurement*: At this stage, there is little or no strategic involvement from procurement, and the function is not seen as strategically important for the organization. The procurement

function is decentralized and characterized by a focus on serving basic needs for materials and services. The main activities involve processing orders and chasing suppliers, and decisions have a short-term impact. Pressure is centred mainly on reducing purchasing prices, and the potential contribution of procurement to organizational effectiveness is minimal.

For organizations at this stage of maturity, procurement personnel require clerical and basic IT skills to allow them to interact with internal customers and suppliers. There is limited emphasis on professional development.

To move to the next stage of development needs a more centralized function within the organization, which can leverage procurement spend and deliver greater savings. A broader perspective on total cost, focusing not only on purchasing price, can also lead to better results and more significant influence within the organization.

2 *Cost-driven procurement*: The procurement function has strategic intent, but it's not necessarily aligned closely with the strategy of the organization. For organizations at this stage, the procurement function has an analytical approach focused on minimizing costs. This approach involves achieving better deals from suppliers and streamlining business processes. The more advanced organizations in this category take a more holistic view of cost and use tools such as spend analysis and total cost of ownership (TCO). Procurement's contribution to performance is mainly in terms of savings.

Procurement professionals in organizations at this stage tend to have strong analytical skills that allow them to analyse spend and evaluate the return on investments. They also have good negotiation and contracting skills to be able to get the best deals from suppliers.

The impact of procurement on the bottom line should not be underestimated. However, if organizations want to shift to the next maturity stage, they need a change in mindset, from a cost focus to a wider set of financial and non-financial measures including risk, value, innovation and growth. This will, in turn, shift procurement's influence from cost reduction to value creation.

3 *Integrated procurement*: Procurement has a clear strategy that is aligned with that of the organization. The focus at this stage is on integrating and aligning strategies and processes with stakeholders across the supply chain, including internal and external customers and suppliers. To do so, organizations establish a portfolio of relationships with different stakeholders. The main contribution is in creating value for the customer and generating additional revenue.

Procurement professionals operating in organizations at this level need to master the management of complexity and require not only analytical and negotiation skills but also emotional and relational skills that allow them to influence others inside and outside their organization.

The shift to procurement leadership involves a radical change in the procurement role within the organization and an even greater change in its role with suppliers. Procurement needs to move from aligning with the strategy towards formulating strategy in sync with other functions.

4 *Leading procurement*: At this stage, the procurement function is actively engaged in shaping strategy, transforming its organization and leading the supply base to search for sustainable competitive advantage. Procurement leaders do not only align their strategy with the rest of the organization but also shape strategy by creating a vision that contributes to the success of their organization and the entire supply chain (see Flex case study).

At this stage, procurement professionals require an extensive set of transformational, visioning and influencing skills. They need to convince their internal colleagues of the power of procurement and align their suppliers to create stronger supply chains.

The four stages in the maturity model represent progress towards a more efficient and effective procurement function, providing a competitive advantage to the organization. However, it is essential to remember that the maturity model is a broad generalization and that many contextual factors, such as the maturity of the industry, the size of the organization, the power balance with customers and suppliers, and the overall economic situation, might affect the role and influence procurement can have in an organization.

TABLE 1.1 Procurement maturity model

	Transactional	Cost-driven	Integrated	Leading
Alignment/ involvement in strategy	• No strategic orientation or involvement	• Independent from organization's strategy	• Supports organizational strategy • Close alignment	• Influences organizational strategy • Provides strong input to values and strategies • Move from strategic sourcing to SRM
Scope of activities	• Clerical in nature • One-off negotiations with suppliers • Order processing • Hardly any tendering	• Commercial activities • Tendering • Negotiation • Getting the deal!	• Active in make-buy decisions • Outsourcing • Global sourcing • Focus on strategic sourcing • Relationship management and supplier development	• End-to-end supply chain management • Few areas of external spend untouched • Relationship management and supplier development
Relationship management (external and internal)	• No supplier relationship management (SRM) • No engagement with other functions	• Limited SRM • Moderate integration with internal functions	• Portfolio approach to relationships • Engagement in SRM • Extensive internal integration	• Seen as customer of choice by suppliers • Engage with other stakeholders • Close internal alignment
Use of technology	• Ad hoc use of IT • Use of spreadsheets	• Automation of clerical activities to reduce cost	• Investments in ICT • E-procurement	• Extensive use of e-procurement + internet technologies
Skills and knowledge of people	• Clerical • Technical skill gaps • Some training provided	• Technical competence • Negotiation and commercial skills • Training provided	• Professionalized • Highly technical competence • Good project management skills • Systematic integration of training plans	• Professionalized • Highly technical competence • Transformational and leadership skills • Continuous development • Attracts top talent

(continued)

TABLE 1.1 (Continued)

	Transactional	Cost-driven	Integrated	Leading
Performance measurement (KPIs)	• No structured targets and limited follow-up • Focus on number of purchase orders handled, volume metrics and order process compliance	• Targets and reviews focus on financial results • Focus on price reductions and contract coverage	• Balanced scorecard • Focus on total cost of ownership (TCO) and business alignment	• Comprehensive balanced scorecard • Continuous monitoring • Focus on TCO, innovation, sustainability and continuous improvement
How visible is procurement?	• Not prominent	• Elevated profile based on savings potential	• Highly visible internally and externally	• Internally procurement is seen as a driver of competitive advantage • Supply chain champion

SOURCES Burt and Doyle (1993); Cousins et al (2006); Freeman and Cavinato (1990); Reck and Long (1988); Schiele (2007)

CASE STUDY
The LIVING supply chain at Flex

Flex is a multinational technological manufacturer, involved in the design, manufacture and distribution of products for other companies, including Apple, Google, Ford and Nike. The company employs over 200,000 people, has manufacturing sites in over 30 countries, and manages a global network of more than 14,000 suppliers.

Flex has invested heavily in developing a software system called Pulse to coordinate such a complex supply chain. The system integrates data from over 50 different information feeds, including internal data sources (eg inventory, manufacturing, transportation) and external sources (eg news feeds, Twitter, fire departments, police scanners). Pulse allows Flex's staff to monitor and analyse 'big data' using apps on their phones.

Flex has also built a physical network of Pulse centres, where active tracking of over 1,000 supply chains is done 24/7. Currently, they have Pulse centres in the United States, Israel, China, India, Mexico, Poland and Austria.

Many companies have tried to create centrally managed control towers for their supply chains. Instead, Flex's approach has been to democratize information, by making it available to all relevant staff, so that they can make swift decisions, and react promptly to potential risks.

Tom Linton, their former chief procurement and supply chain officer, asserts: 'Before the availability of these tools, it was like driving on a motorway in your car and trying to monitor and increase your speed using yesterday's speedometer information. It's almost a cliché to say that the pace of change is accelerating, but it's true. Digital allows supply chains to keep up and often drive that speed' (Henderson, 2017).

Linton has a philosophy for running the supply chain. He calls it the LIVING supply chain, an acronym that stands for:

Live – make real-time information transparent
Interactive – make information interactive across federated supply networks
Velocity – move assets faster and protect working capital
Intelligent – provide descriptive and predictive analytics
Networked – connect the network of partners that co-evolves and co-innovates
Good – create a supply chain that balances economic, environmental and social
   factors

By allowing their supply chain to move faster, Flex have removed five days of inventory from their supply chain, improving cash flow, boosting operating margins, and improving customer service.

SOURCES   Flex (2018); Handfield & Linton (2017); Henderson (2017)

The context of strategic procurement

Strategic procurement is a process that connects organizational strategy with day-to-day procurement operations. It aims to lead the supply base to contribute to the organization's strategy and create competitive advantage. The challenge is to develop a procurement strategy that on the one hand is in line with the organization's strategy and on the other faces the coalface of procurement, and the different categories and markets in which it operates.

Figure 1.3 presents the activity for formulating and delivering a procurement strategy as part of three cycle processes. The *business strategy cycle* is the process of creating a vision, goals and strategy for the organization, implementing them and learning from them. The

FIGURE 1.3   Strategic procurement in context

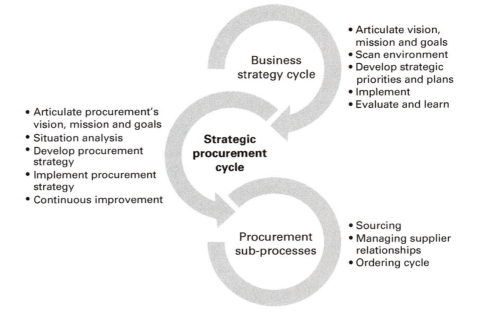

• Articulate vision, mission and goals
• Scan environment
• Develop strategic priorities and plans
• Implement
• Evaluate and learn

Business strategy cycle

• Articulate procurement's vision, mission and goals
• Situation analysis
• Develop procurement strategy
• Implement procurement strategy
• Continuous improvement

Strategic procurement cycle

Procurement sub-processes

• Sourcing
• Managing supplier relationships
• Ordering cycle

strategic procurement cycle, which is at the core of this book, represents the process of developing and delivering on the procurement
strategy. And the *procurement sub-processes* represent the tactical
and operational activities of sourcing, managing supplier relationships and processing the order cycle. All three cycles use feedback as
a continuous improvement mechanism, but they also feed into each
other, providing alignment across the organizational hierarchy.

While the arrows in Figure 1.3 indicate a general flow from organizational strategy, through procurement strategy and into buying,
they also imply a feedback flow in which the day-to-day realities of
the buying process can affect procurement strategy. In turn, procurement strategy can influence organizational strategy.

CASE STUDY

IKEA responding to challenges in the supply base

IKEA provides a good example of an organization that has adapted its strategy in
response to challenges in the supply base. IKEA is one of the world's largest
buyers of wood, and in 2020 they consumed 19 million cubic metres of wood.
This represents about 1 per cent of the world's supply.

While wood is a renewable raw material, it takes a long time to replace a tree.
This presents IKEA and its suppliers with a challenge that is both environmental
and economic. In response, they have developed a sustainability strategy with
clear goals and responsibilities.

In 2012 IKEA set a target to source 100 per cent of their wood sustainably by
2020, promoting sustainable forestry methods across the industry and
contributing to ending deforestation. In their most recent press release, they
claim that in 2020 more than 98 per cent of the wood they use is FSC-certified
or recycled. While this is a formidable achievement, they also acknowledge that
because of disruptions and new suppliers, they cannot guarantee a 100 per cent
fulfilment of their original goal.

As part of this strategy, they have invested in sustainable forests, established
clear forestry requirements, developed a code of conduct for suppliers called the
IWAY, and implemented comprehensive audit and transparency procedures
across the supply chain. Furthermore, they have engaged stakeholders such as
the Forest Stewardship Council (FSC) and the World Wide Fund for Nature
(WWF) to gain legitimacy and ensure they address wider concerns.

SOURCES Gorman (2013); IKEA (2016, 2021); Kelly (2012)

Much has been written about business strategy formulation and about the buying process; the cog at the centre of this process, the strategic procurement cycle, has received far less attention. This book aims to fill this gap by providing a deep dive into the different aspects of strategic procurement.

Procurement sub-processes and the road to maturity

If the purpose of the procurement process is to help ensure 'supply' in the 'supply chain', how is that achieved? Essentially there are three procurement sub-processes to consider, as shown in Figure 1.4. After specifying needs for supplies, there is a supply market search for the supplies that are needed. This is followed by the selection of supplies and the firms who make them. After this process, the suppliers have been contracted, but they have not yet delivered the physical goods. For this, we have the operational process in which supplies are ordered and received, and suppliers are paid for their services.

In Figure 1.4, procurement sub-processes are shown as interlinked circular processes. On the right are the operational procurement activities that focus on placing orders, receiving goods and paying invoices. For these processes to run smoothly, automation through enterprise resource planning (ERP) or e-procurement tools is often valuable. But aligning procurement processes with suppliers can be even more valuable, linking ordering systems on the 'buy' side with shipment systems on the 'supply' side. Thus, IT systems help to reduce errors, accelerate shipments and reduce transaction costs. Managerial integration can create even greater benefits. This type of integration takes time, effort and investment and, as a result, it cannot be achieved with all suppliers. So focal firms contract with selected suppliers and agree upon product and service catalogues (middle cog, Figure 1.4) so that – in the operational process – not every purchase needs to be treated as a new one. Buyers can order from selected and pre-qualified suppliers so that they do not have to find fresh sources and negotiate new commercial terms for every order.

FIGURE 1.4 Three main sub-processes of procurement

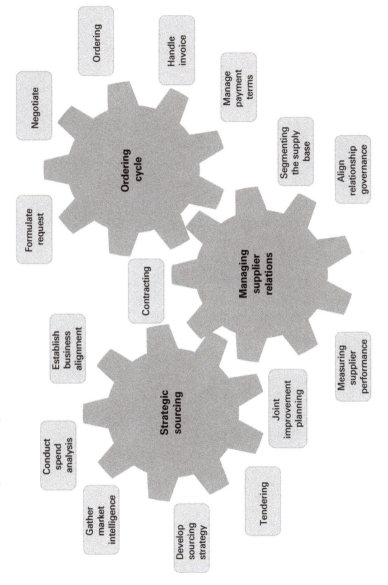

Aligning contract and catalogue management means that the left-hand cog in Figure 1.4 is needed – strategic sourcing. Suppliers are selected and contracted for longer-term relationships in a particular area of spend. But prior to that, the company's need for procured products and services is assessed in depth, its current spend with suppliers in each area of spend is assessed, the supplier market is studied, and a strategy to meet business needs by means of a procurement strategy is developed. Typically, this strategy is developed by a team of buyers but includes business users and stakeholders such as manufacturing. Often senior management is asked to sponsor and sign off on strategies. In short, there is a lot that happens before procurement actions such as tendering for framework agreements even begins. Development of a strategy for a given category of spend might lead to the conclusion that the category would be better made in-house, and so should not be tendered at all. The result of the strategic sourcing process typically is the appointment of suppliers whose contracts are used in tactical procurement (production planning, project sourcing, etc) and operational procurement. Based upon tactical and operational experiences with contracted suppliers, performance is often evaluated and rated. Vendor ratings can then be used as the basis for supplier development and relationship management.

The relative focus of a procurement organization on the three sub-processes in Figure 1.4 can be tied to maturity levels. If procurement is mostly focused on 'procure and pay' and 'operational' activities, then its buyers are more tactical in nature. If a focal firm allocates staff and time to activities more to the left, it can be expected to see greater returns on its efforts and have the opportunity to align procurement more deeply with strategies and drivers of customer value. Staff focused mostly on operational procurement activities will allocate little time to strategic sourcing and supplier relationship activities, whereas staff focused on the left should not be allocating too much time to ordering, pricing orders, and tracing shipments and payments. If this is the case, the lack of balance across the three processes can lead to tensions, inefficiencies and even undermine the value that procurement can deliver.

Structure of the book

The book is structured into four main parts, as depicted in Figure 1.5. Part One, which includes this introductory chapter, is dedicated to procurement strategy and structure. This first chapter sets the scene and explains why procurement is becoming more important and how it can lead to sustainable competitive advantage. Chapter 2 discusses how procurement fits in the organizational structure and how it needs to align its goals, both across organizational layers and throughout interorganizational supply chain processes. Chapter 3 concentrates on the strategic procurement cycle, discussing every stage of the process and presenting tools and techniques that can be useful at each stage, such as supply market intelligence, spend analysis and portfolio analysis.

Part Two explores the role of procurement in the supply network. Chapter 4 focuses on supplier relationship management, looking at how to establish the appropriate relationships with suppliers and how to get the best performance from them. Chapter 5 concentrates

FIGURE 1.5 Structure of the book

PART ONE Procurement strategy	• 1. Introduction: the strategic role of procurement • 2. Procurement and the organization • 3. The strategic procurement cycle
PART TWO Procurement and the supply network	• 4. Supplier relationship management • 5. Global sourcing
PART THREE Delivering performance in procurement	• 6. Strategic cost management • 7. The impact of procurement on financial results • 8. Supply chain risk management • 9. Digitization of procurement
PART FOUR Sustaining procurement performance	• 10. Sustainable procurement • 11. The future of procurement

on the global sourcing phenomenon, exploring its benefits and risks and providing insights into how to establish and manage a global supply network.

In Part Three, we turn to the different aspects of procurement performance. First, Chapter 6 concentrates on strategic cost management and how cost management can become a strategic weapon for the organization. This chapter also provides several tools that can be useful in understanding and managing costs. Chapter 7 elaborates on the relationship between procurement and financial performance by focusing on the topic of supply chain finance. Chapter 8 focuses on another important aspect of procurement performance, namely risk management. This chapter explains why supply chains are becoming riskier and what companies can do to manage and mitigate the impact of risks, such as the COVID-19 pandemic. In Chapter 9, we turn to the digitization of procurement, where we explore the role of technology in driving efficiency and effectiveness in procurement processes.

Part Four focuses on how to sustain procurement performance. Chapter 10 looks into the environmental and social challenges facing procurement and provides tools to manage and ultimately gain competitive advantage from these issues. Finally, Chapter 11 presents insights into what the future of the procurement profession might look like.

Summary and conclusions

Procurement is central to organizational performance. It can contribute to cost savings, but it can also contribute to other critical performance areas such as flexibility, quality, reliability, innovation, sustainability and resilience. However, its impact is limited by the level of maturity of the function. The four-stage procurement maturity model described in this chapter provides a path to help procurement professionals develop their function to gain impact and influence.

A procurement strategy needs to be aligned both with the organization's strategy and with the processes cutting across interorganizational boundaries. In this chapter, we have presented a model that describes how to formulate, implement and execute a procurement strategy that delivers on its promise of being both strategic and influential.

If procurement leaders are to have a seat at the boardroom table, they need to understand and demonstrate the impact they can have in delivering value to the organization and show they can collaborate both internally and externally to deliver mutually beneficial results.

References

Barney, J B (1991) Firm resources and sustained competitive advantage, *Journal of Management*, **17**, pp 99–120

Barney, J B (1995) Looking inside for competitive advantage, *Academy of Management Executive*, **9** (4), pp 49–61

Burt, D N and Doyle, M F (1993) *The American Keiretsu: a strategic weapon for global competitiveness,* Irwin, Homewood, IL

Cammish, R and Keough, M (1991) A strategic role for purchasing, *The McKinsey Quarterly*, **3**, pp 22–39

CAPS (2017) *Cross-Industry Report of Standard Benchmarks – 2017*, CAPS Research, Tempe, AZ

Cousins, P D, Lawson, B and Squire, B (2006) An empirical taxonomy of purchasing functions, *International Journal of Operations & Production Management*, **26** (7) pp 775–94

Dyer, J H and Singh, H (1998) The relational view: cooperative strategy and sources of interorganizational competitive advantage, *Academy of Management Review*, **23**, pp 660–79

Flex (2018) How we use real-time data analytics to manage complex supply chains, https://flex.com/resources/how-we-use-real-time-data-analytics-to-manage-complex-supply-chains (archived at https://perma.cc/L2UU-PMP6)

Freeman, V T and Cavinato, J L (1990) Fitting purchasing to the strategic firm: frameworks, processes, and values, *Journal of Purchasing & Materials Management*, **26** (4) pp 6–10

Gorman, R (2013) IKEA uses a staggering 1% of the world's wood every year, *Daily Mail*, 6 July

Handfield, R and Linton, T (2017) *The LIVING supply chain: The involving imperative of operating in real time*, John Wiley & Sons, Hoboken, NJ

Henderson, J (2017) Interview: Flex's Tom Linton and the digital supply chain, *Supply Chain Digital*, 9 September, www.supplychaindigital.com/technology/interview-flexs-tom-linton-and-digital-supply-chain (archived at https://perma.cc/GA7H-2YZH)

Hogg, R (2016) Tesla's supply chain set for a surge, *Automotive Logistics*, 26 July, http://automotivelogistics.media/intelligence/teslas-supply-chain-set-surge (archived at https://perma.cc/XSX9-WY8L)

IKEA (2016) IKEA Group Sustainability Report FY16, https://www.ingka.com/wp-content/uploads/2020/01/IKEA-Group-Yearly-Summary-FY16.pdf (archived at https://perma.cc/A7CY-GZWR)

IKEA (2021) Our view on forestry, 24 January, https://about.ikea.com/en/about-us/our-view-on/our-view-on-forestry (archived at https://perma.cc/D96A-7723)

Kelly, A (2012) Ikea to go 'forest positive – but serious challenges lie ahead, *Guardian*, 14 December

Kraljic, P (1983) Purchasing must become supply management, *Harvard Business Review*, **61** (5), pp 109–17

Lavie, D (2006) The competitive advantage of interconnected firms: an extension of the resource-based view, *Academy of Management Review*, **31**, pp 638–58

Reck, R F and Long, B G (1988) Purchasing: a competitive weapon, *Journal of Purchasing & Materials Management*, **24** (3), pp 2–8

Schiele, H (2007) Supply-management maturity, cost savings and purchasing absorptive capacity: testing the procurement–performance link, *Journal of Purchasing and Supply Management*, **13**, pp 274–93

Tesla (2014) Panasonic and Tesla sign agreement for the Gigafactory, 30 July, https://www.tesla.com/blog/panasonic-and-tesla-sign-agreement-gigafactory (archived at https://perma.cc/6XAC-U9PQ)

Tesla (2020) About Tesla, https://www.tesla.com/about (archived at https://perma.cc/394A-M5N8)

Toolan, D (2016) Without supplier innovation Tesla would have built another Camry, *Vizibl*, 19 May, http://blog.vizibl.co/without-supplier-innovation-tesla-would-have-built-a-camry (archived at https://perma.cc/T9Q6-LJSE)

Wade, M and Hulland, J (2004) The resource-based view and information systems research: review, extension, and suggestions for future research, *MIS Quarterly*, **28** (1), pp 107–42

Wernle, B (2015) Suppliers give Tesla high praise for innovation, *Automotive News*, 9 November, http://www.autonews.com/article/20151109/OEM10/311099941/suppliers-give-tesla-high-praise-for-innovation (archived at https://perma.cc/K6CD-STVH)

02

Procurement and the organization

Organizing for success

REMKO VAN HOEK

While in theory any organizational structure can work for procurement there are specific considerations in organizational design that make it worthy of attention. Procurement teams do not operate in a vacuum and need to work with peer functions or business units whose money they are helping spend wisely. This means that the organizational structure needs to support that. Procurement reporting lines upward and within the procurement department matter not only for the alignment with the business but also for target setting and proximity to key stakeholders (for example, it might help to have reporting lines into the business to help focus procurement on alignment). Finally, roles and responsibilities between procurement and the business are important for procurement success. Since procurement is often positioned as a business partner and an 'internal service' it is key that there is clarity about 'who does what' throughout the core procurement processes.

This chapter is structured as follows: the next section introduces basic organization forms used for procurement organizations and their respective pros and cons. Next, the critical internal need for internal alignment between the procurement function and its colleagues in the business is considered as a key area to 'put the organizational structure to work' and a framework for assessing and driving internal alignment is introduced. The final section considers roles and responsibilities for procurement and its colleagues in the business.

Procurement organization structures

Prior to procurement's rise to prominence going back a decade (or two to three, depending upon what organization you look at), it used not to be much of an organization on its own. Procurement was largely an administrative or business support functionality focusing on ensuring supplies, processing purchase orders and once in a while negotiating a discount. Buyers were generally tucked away at the back of the factory and not really organized as a function.

With the discovery of procurement as a function that can help strategically source areas of external spend, consolidate and coordinate spend across factories and businesses, and pay for itself multiple times over, this has changed. In most mid- to large-size organizations a case has long been made for investing in procurement capability, leadership and development of a function and a department. The business case for this is often based upon the opportunity to better organize and coordinate external spend, to improve leverage in contracting and negotiating, and to form a more orchestrated face to the supply base.

CASE STUDY
John Deere

At John Deere, the farming equipment manufacturer from the United States, the case for investment in procurement was illustrated by showing the board how many different gloves were used in factories across its global network of operations. All had the same quality level and standards, but they were bought decentrally by uncoordinated (part-time) buyers who (when adding it all up) actually spent a lot of company time on this. The case was simple: why not have one capable buyer do this once and for all, to save time, to ensure quality standards, streamline the interface with the supply base and get a much better deal on the supplies. It did not take the board long to identify dozens of other and more important areas to seek out similar benefits.

With this recognition of procurement came the need and the opportunity to organize procurement as a function and a department. Since the late 1980s there has been an ongoing wave of procurement directors and chief procurement officers being hired and appointed as direct reports of C-level executives. And these have been supported by lots of benchmarks on how to structure and size their organizations. Typical measures considered include the amount of external spend per buyer, number of business entities with unique buying needs, or number of spend categories with different supply-market dynamics (often buyers are allocated to areas of spend or business areas, so diversity of businesses and spend areas drive the complexity of buying).

Procurement reporting lines

Heads of procurement and their teams can be found to report into different parts of the C-suite. A common reporting line is into the chief financial officer (CFO) because of procurement's obvious ability to drive costs down and support P&L improvement efforts. Reporting to the CFO can be helpful for procurement, as CFOs can steward procurement into the business as a go-to function to help the business hit budget targets. Procurement can also report into the supply chain or operations organization; this holds particular benefits in an organization that is heavily operations-focused with a high purchased-in value, and supplies and suppliers that are critical to ensuring delivery accuracy and efficiency. While less common, procurement can also report to the CEO of the organization. This is beneficial because of the CEO's big stick and overall perspective, and it can help procurement broaden its contribution to multiple strategic priorities.

CASE STUDY
Note from the author

As a three times chief procurement officer (CPO)/procurement director across very different industries, I have reported to the CFO, the CEO and the chief supply chain officer (CSCO). There are noticeable differences in direction and focus between these top executives, and this impacts what is asked of procurement and the CPO. Reporting to the CFO works well at the time that procurement is driving savings and strategic sourcing and trying to make the business case for procurement work. The CFO can open a lot of doors to spend pools and budget holders, either as a suggestion, as a mandate or as part of the budget process. Reporting to the CEO can open procurement and the CPO to a broader agenda, and this works best if the case for procurement on savings has been proven and procurement is ready to do more than strategic sourcing. So, while reporting to the CEO enables broadening scope and impact, it does require strategic capability.

Reporting to the CSCO sets procurement up well for a more holistic involvement in supply chain management. This will likely make it easier to support key topics such as sustainability and risk management in the supply chain, topics that we will discuss in later chapters. It certainly also makes it easier for procurement to avoid a too-narrow focus on purchase price only. Obviously, not every company has an integrated supply chain organization (and more should), and in some industries there may not be much of a need for such an organization (think of banks or consulting firms, for example). This makes procurement a unique part of the supply chain; while not all companies have a supply chain, all companies do have external spend and relevance for a procurement function.

All these considerations reinforce the relevance of developing an operating model and organizational design for procurement that works well for the company and its industry. In this process, there are no universal solutions.

Three models

Table 2.1 compares three typical organizational structures. The decentralized structure at the top of the chart was most common in the past and is used in organizations where procurement is not really organized as a function. As a result, there is no leverage across businesses, and there is not a real ability to manage spend areas as such; the focus is on supporting the local business needs without much scope for investment in the development of buyers and the procurement team, because of its small, operational and local focus. The latter can represent a benefit of this structure; proximity to local business issues and markets, and visibility locally of procurement's contribution. This structure is used least frequently by modern and advanced procurement functions today, when compared to the two alternative structures, as its downsides outweigh its benefits. Its benefits can also be retained in the centre-led organizational model.

The centre-led structure supplements local buyers and teams with a small corporate team, headed by a senior procurement leader, consisting of category managers or lead buyers. While the senior procurement leader provides functional leadership to the entire procurement organization, only the corporate team has a direct reporting line into this leader. The local buyers and team will report to a manager in the business, possibly with a dotted secondary reporting line into the central procurement leader. The role of the central team of category managers or lead buyers is to leverage spend across business units and local teams into coordinated spend pools and categories, and to develop strategies and strategic sourcing initiatives for categories of spend, as well as presenting one face to critical suppliers. This represents a serious commitment to developing the procurement function that brings a lot of added benefits to local teams, including investment in the function, new best practices and a central team that helps get more out of local spend across the company. The centre-led model is often used in organizations where there is a legacy of local teams that report to local businesses. The board investment in procurement is planted on top and in addition to that. This structure does have some potential tension built into it if locally optimized buying might not match 100 per cent with globally optimized buying. In particular, when local businesses are under pressure and consider the buyers in their organization as 'theirs' this introduces tension in the procurement organization between the 'local heroes who know their business best and have done this well for a long time' and the 'corporate people who are planted in the corporate centre – really smart but further removed'.

This tension is why boards sometimes choose to have all buyers reporting centrally into the office of the chief procurement officer (CPO). This holds the benefit of strong alignment between buyers in different parts of the organization and makes it easier to coordinate well and create a one-team approach to maximize procurement impact. The risk in this structure, of course, is that buyers end up

TABLE 2.1 Typical procurement organization structure

Type of organization	Description	Pros	Cons	Central procurement control	Local P&L responsibility
Decentralized	Procurement takes place in local businesses with no corporate role	Local control and autonomy Embedded in the business Flat organization structure with clear accountability Good match to local supply-based and service	No volume leverage No sharing of practices Duplication of efforts Reduced ability to invest in people and technology for professionalization	Low	High
Centre-led	Small central team for category strategy and supplier segmentation Local buyers in the business report dotted line into procurement	Ability to achieve leverage by establishing collaboration across businesses Limited overhead costs and Proximity to the local business maintained Ability to share best practices and learn from each other	Requires stronger leadership to ensure local buyers engage May take longer to professionalize and achieve results Because businesses can 'opt out' results may only be achieved partially	Medium	Medium
Centralized	Central procurement organization for all spend and all buyers report into the procurement function	Maximum corporate leverage Easiest to streamline procurement process and develop once for all Ability to professionalize procurement	Procurement more removed from the business Lowered local responsiveness Risk of overhead and central bureaucracy	High	Low

removed from local buying needs and operational considerations. So for a central structure to not turn into a 'corporate waterhead', it is key that buyers stay connected to stakeholders they are working with and for in the business, and that they not only spend time there but also really work on embedding themselves into different functions.

Five additional considerations about organizational structures:

1 Reporting line, not location – the differences between the three types of organizational structures reflect differences in reporting lines; to the business, dotted line or hard line into the function. Do not confuse this with location. While in the centralized structure, buyers all report to a manager in the procurement function; they are not necessarily all located in the corporate head office. In fact, it makes sense to locate (some) buyers in this structure in business locations; it can help reduce the risk of being removed from the business.

2 Culture is key – on top of the organizational considerations surrounding the organizational structures – do not ignore company culture. If a company is very focused on local decision making and local operating structures implementing a centralized model, even when sensible from a procurement perspective, may put a wedge between procurement and its business partners.

3 Don't go against the operating model of the business – equally so, if a company is very centralized throughout its organization, choosing a decentralized structure for procurement might lead to alignment challenges between procurement and the colleagues in the business that it needs work with (we will discuss alignment with the business further in the next section).

4 Change over time – as procurement teams mature, and businesses and markets change, the best organizational structure may change over time.

5 All can work, nothing might work – having been part of procurement organizations of all three types, it is my experience that all can work with the right leadership and efforts of procurement teams to align with the wider business. And all can fail without effort to drive alignment. So while an important choice to make, picking the right organizational structure on its own is no guarantee for success in procurement.

CASE STUDY
Webhelp

Webhelp is a fast-growing customer contact company based in Europe that is active in over 30 countries with over 150 centres and 50,000 staff. The company operates customer contact centres for its customers across a number of industries.

When the CFO of the company initiated a corporate performance improvement programme, procurement was included as one of the tracks in that programme. This set procurement up well to explore opportunities to organize for greater business contribution. The programme was CFO-driven, had board support and its steering committee involved C-level executives from around the company.

During a period of a few months of procurement opportunity assessment, the team involved in the programme conducted spend analysis, worked with country teams to identify and prioritize procurement opportunities, and ran pilot sourcing projects in selected high-potential high-return IT and facility spend categories. Based upon this experience, the initial results, and the long list of opportunities for more effective procurement and strategic sourcing, an organizational model was proposed to the board in order to organize for ongoing success.

Because the company is very decentralized in its organization and has a culture of strong local autonomy and decision making, a centralized organizational structure was not even considered an option; it would have put procurement at odds with the company culture and the ways of working throughout the company. Instead, the company selected a centre-led model, as it found this would combine the ability to aggregate spend and implement more strategic sourcing approaches across countries, with the retention of local autonomy and agility while avoiding too much of an increase in corporate overheads and policy.

Internal alignment as a prerequisite for procurement impact

A primary operating principle in procurement touches upon the work that an organization needs to do internally, before it turns to the supply base. If not working closely aligned with the business, procurement might be sourcing supplies that are not fully right for business needs, running the risk of focusing on the wrong supplies, wasting supplier time and credibility internally, as well as company credibility in the supply market. In short, procurement is spending the business's budget, not its own, and it needs to make sure it is not negotiating a great deal for something that is just not needed. If procurement's role is to assure the inbound flow of materials, it is important for procurement professionals to be closely aligned with their peers in the supply chain. Without that, it will be hard to know exactly what to buy and what opportunities in the supply market are most valid to consider. Achieving this alignment takes consistent effort, much of it on the part of procurement professionals themselves.

How is alignment achieved in procurement? It is achieved at a number of stages, times and levels. Business plan alignment is achieved around the annual business planning and review cycle at a senior level between business unit management and procurement leadership. Alignment around specific business objectives that need to be addressed can be achieved through cross-functional operation of a project team. Coordination around specific contracts can be regulated by ordering policies and spend authorization procedures, which specify that orders over a certain value need to be co-signed by procurement.

Alignment needs to be achieved through all three core procurement processes. In strategic sourcing, it is key for procurement to partner with colleagues in the business to get the specifications and sourcing strategy focused on the proper business needs. In supplier relationship management, procurement needs input from the business to be able to provide feedback on supplier performance, and business leaders need to engage in identifying relevant performance improvement opportunities. In the ordering cycle, the business needs to request and leadership needs to approve spend.

Achieving internal alignment requires of procurement professionals:

- the ability to identify potential levers for alignment and for spotting business needs;
- willingness to see functional expertise as a price of entry, not a differentiator: as peers expect you to be knowledgeable about procurement, that is not a likely subject of conversation – business needs are;

- adopting a service focus to centre efforts around business needs, not around procurement's desire to drive value;
- flexibility in articulating the agenda differently depending upon business needs, and creativity to find a way to stick to the agenda, despite different business needs;
- the ability to 'sell' ideas through participation rather than through the use of authority or position (again, asking for that is a sign of reluctance to engage);
- standing strong on business values, such as 'customers first, positions last'; 'improvement forever, complacency never'; 'value centricity, position focus eccentricity' to help keep the discussion focused.

Ways to achieve alignment include:

- embedding/stationing key procurement staff in the businesses to make the part of the business 'fabric';
- using metrics of the business to evaluate performance;
- studying business plans and business training material;
- interviewing executives, getting invited to business meetings to understand the agenda of priorities and issues.

Markers of aligned procurement organizations include:

- strong business partner focus among staff;
- incentives and performance indicators that are not solely financial – such as cost savings based on purchase price variance (PPV) – the 'standard cost' that has been budgeted and then used as a measure of procurement's performance, which ignores other performance measures, such as those based on quality and delivery reliability;
- results are not claimed by procurement, but procurement contributions are referenced in business results (annual reports, for example);
- procedures and spend authorization processes exist but are hardly referenced, due to seamless working relationships in which peers acknowledge each other's roles and have clarity about roles and responsibilities.

Alignment triad

This section so far has focused on internal alignment between procurement and peer functions as a prerequisite for success. Growing C-suite sponsorship for procurement contributions to enterprise value creation is a certain positive factor for the future of the discipline; it also means that procurement professionals now need to align horizontally with the business but also vertically with C-level executives. As a result, in the future internal alignment needs to be achieved in a triad interrelation between the supply chain, the business and the board.

Figure 2.1 shows a grid that categorizes alignment between procurement and the CEO/board. The top-right quadrant covers areas or initiatives where there is a clear alignment between the priorities of the CEO and those of procurement. These are the top priority areas where procurement has to deliver results; cost savings are the clear example of a priority area in this quadrant. The top-left corner includes areas where procurement would like to contribute, but the CEO does not perceive a major impact. In these areas, we might find talent management and supplier relationship management where procurement perceive they can make a difference, but have so far failed to make the case to the CEO. These areas require a 'sell and tell' approach, as well as the use of pilot projects to demonstrate the value to the organization. The bottom-right quadrant includes areas that the CEO emphasizes, but procurement fails to see their impact. Finally, the bottom-left corner refers to activities where neither the CEO nor procurement places high importance.

Aligning priorities between procurement and the CEO is only the first step in the process of alignment, as in order to deliver performance, aligning with the rest of the business is just as important. To incorporate this into the model, we have split each of the quadrants into two halves representing alignment (or misalignment) between procurement and their peers in the business, as can be seen in Figure 2.2.

The top-right corner is split into 'Bull's eye' and 'Delivery pitfalls'. *Bull's eye* are those areas or initiatives where all three parties concur on their high priority and agree they should be the main focus. *Delivery pitfalls* are areas or initiatives where there is support from the CEO, but some business resistance exists. In these

FIGURE 2.1 Procurement: CEO alignment matrix

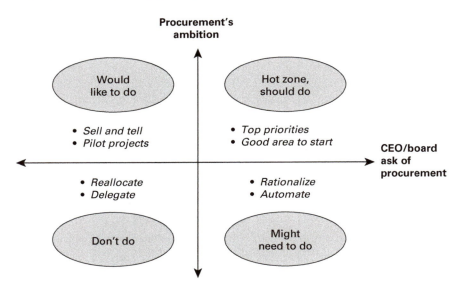

cases, procurement professionals can rely on their CEO to try to persuade business colleagues and align performance measures to gain their support, but they also need to watch out that they do not commit to objectives set by the CEO too quickly as they might run into real resistance in implementation in the business. The top-left quadrant is divided into 'Business-led' and 'Ivory tower risk'. *Business-led* refers to those areas that both procurement and the organization prioritize, but are not perceived as central to the CEO. Here procurement teams can collaborate with the rest of the organization to make things work and show results, letting the business sing their praises to gain CEO approval. *Ivory towers* are perceived as highly important for procurement, but neither the CEO nor the business finds them important. In these cases, procurement teams have to be careful not to embark on pet projects, and if they decide to pursue these initiatives, they should closely monitor performance and communicate results to persuade other stakeholders. The bottom right quadrant is divided into 'Need to do' and 'Potential binds'. *Need to do* are those areas or initiatives that the

CEO and the business consider important, but procurement does not. These are areas where procurement teams need to support but should not take a leading role and, if possible, automate. *Potential binds* are areas the CEO prioritizes, but neither the business nor procurement consider important. In these cases, there is a risk of being caught between fires, and procurement should try to work with other areas of the business to make a case for a change in priorities from the CEO. Finally, the bottom-left quadrant is divided into 'Challenges' and 'No-brainers'. *Challenges* are those initiatives that the business wants to pursue despite lack of support from the CEO and where procurement does not perceive value. In these cases, procurement should try to persuade colleagues about the return on investment or give them the opportunity to pursue their initiatives without major input from procurement teams.

FIGURE 2.2   Alignment triad

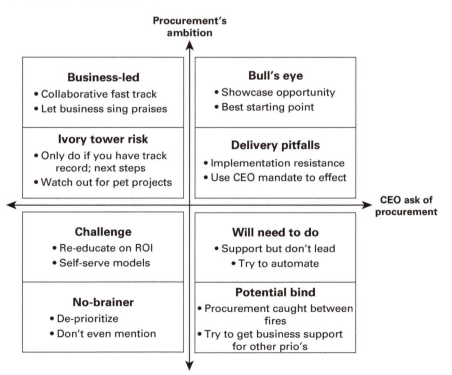

No-brainers are those initiatives that receive no support from the business and should be de-prioritized and, if possible, abandoned.

In summary, alignment across business, functions and hierarchies has long been acknowledged as an antecedent for procurement performance. In this section, we expanded the thinking about internal alignment to a triadic perspective. Given procurement's rise on the CEO's list of contributors to its strategic agenda, this triadic perspective is becoming more relevant and can be expected to continue to do so in the years to come. As a result, procurement managers will need to incorporate the framework introduced in their strategic planning and initiative prioritization efforts.

Alignment mechanism

Widely used techniques and tools to achieve internal alignment include cross-functional teams, the development of roles and responsibilities, and account planning with the business.

Cross-functional teams

In the strategic sourcing process, there are several key areas where teaming of procurement across functions with peers in the business is critical to achieving several things, including:

- proper specifications of buying needs and requirements from business users and budget holders;
- developing a business-centric and relevant sourcing strategy;
- ensuring buy-in from business users to help drive adoption of sourcing results and outcomes;
- achieving buying process design and implementation that will work.

In practice, this means that strategic sourcing teams will typically bring together procurement professionals and users from the business at the workgroup level, or at least at the specification of needs and evaluation of proposals stages. Business peers are often invited to participate in supplier presentations and discussions to demonstrate to the supply base that the project is not 'procurement in isolation' but a business-centric and relevant effort. Procurement leaders may also seek to install a steering group for strategic sourcing projects that brings together procurement leadership and business leadership for the project team to propose category strategies, evaluation criteria and a supplier selection recommendation. Beyond that, cross functional teaming is not only important for effective strategic sourcing, but also for effective supplier relationship management.

Roles and responsibilities

Table 2.2 details roles and responsibilities in core procurement processes and action areas. This can serve as a template for an organization developing its own version for its procurement function. Three key constituents are involved: the procurement team, peers from relevant business functions and units, and executives that help steer, direct and authorize procurement efforts. These executives will typically include the board sponsor of the procurement function (generally the board executive that procurement reports to) and key business leaders whose spend and business needs are impacted by procurement projects. This can include the chief information officer (CIO) for IT spend, the head of HR for HR projects such as the contracting of recruiting agencies, operations directors for material sourcing projects, the head of marketing for the sourcing of advertising agencies, etc.

In the strategic sourcing process, procurement plays a key role in initiating spend analysis and opportunity identification. The executive team can select priorities and assign the appropriate business team members to projects. These business managers, in turn, may help review the spend analysis for correctness and completeness. Spend analysis tends to provide a rich basis for identifying who to involve and may contain eye-openers for business leaders, for example 'Did you know we work with 50 marketing agencies?' 'Did you know we have three different contracts with one supplier?'

Procurement also will be the main facilitator of the overall sourcing process and lead specific actions, including the development of the sourcing strategy that informs the rest of the project, market engagement through a tender, supplier identification, qualification

TABLE 2.2 Roles and responsibilities in core procurement processes

Core process	Action step	Team member from the business	Procurement	Business executives
	Spend analysis	Review for correctness and completeness	Lead	Assign team
	Set specifications: 'what are we buying?'	Lead	Support	Sign off
	Develop sourcing strategy: 'how are we buying?'	Business need input	Develop	Go/no go
Strategic sourcing	Run tender: 'who are we buying from?'	Support	Lead	Period of radio silence
	Negotiation of terms of what we are buying	Support	Lead	Period of radio silence
	Contracting recommendation	Own	Develop	Decision
	Implementation of new agreement	Lead	Support	Endorse
	Segment suppliers	Business need input	Develop	Sign off
Supplier relationship management	Establish governance model with suppliers	Allocate key contacts	Facilitate	Sign up for resource allocation
	Measure and evaluate supplier performance	Input feedback	Facilitate/develop measurement	Review

(continued)

TABLE 2.2 (Continued)

Core process	Action step	Team member from the business	Procurement	Business executives
Supplier relationship management	Supplier performance-improvement meetings	Own improvement opportunities	Organize meeting and capture improvement opportunities	Meet supplier; focus on identifying (joint) improvement opportunities
	Ongoing collaboration	Lead	Seek joint opportunities and support opportunity capture in collaboration	Foster collaboration focus
	Request purchases	Input	Lead	Review
	Authorize purchases	Possible co-sign	Possible co-sign	Sign off
	Issue purchase orders		Execute	
Ordering cycle	Receive goods	Lead	Record	
	Authorize payment	Possible co-sign	Possible co-sign	Lead
	Execute payment		Execute	

and evaluation, the negotiations stage and the development of a recommendation for supplier selection. Throughout this process, the team members from the business play key roles: they lead the articulation of specifications of what is being bought, and they will be involved throughout the process so that they can lead and own contracting and implementation of the selected suppliers. The sponsoring executives will be asked to sign off on the sourcing strategy, serve as an escalation point in negotiations but otherwise ensure that suppliers do not go around the negotiations team, and they will approve the final supplier selection, and sign and support the contract.

The balance of roles and responsibilities shifts towards the business in the supplier relationship management stage. The business collaborates with suppliers on a day-to-day basis, and it has the responsibility to ensure the operational performance of suppliers. Procurement, however, can bring some process rigour and tools to these efforts and help the business manage enterprise-to-enterprise relationships with key suppliers programmatically. Segmentation of suppliers provides the basis for this, and the segmentation can inform the selection of suppliers to focus on and engage with more strategically and holistically than just in day-to-day operations. This selection would be made by business executives, and procurement can facilitate the establishment of a relationship governance model, the measuring of supplier performance, and the identification and capturing of improvement opportunities with suppliers. Business executives will play a key role in engaging personally with suppliers in meetings and in committing teams and investment to improvement opportunities.

Procurement's involvement in the ordering cycle may be channelled predominantly through a more operational team that processes and executes purchase orders and supplier payments in response to business requests and executive approvals of that spend. This team can be placed close to or with the accounts payable department in the finance function. It is not advisable, however, to remove this team from procurement altogether as it plays a key role in ensuring accurate spend data, adoption of supplier terms and compliance with contracts. Essentially this team provides a foundation for strategic sourcing and the ongoing management of supplier relationships.

Account planning

Account planning is a technique that can help procurement leaders achieve alignment and agreement about priorities and collaboration with the business. In particular, if an account plan for procurement support to a business is developed around the annual business planning process, it can prove an effective way to embed procurement into the business plan and thereby 'make it part of the plan'. It aligns procurement with the business cycle and enables procurement leaders to work with peers in the business to prioritize joint efforts. The account plan can also serve as a basis for mid-year or quarterly reviews of progress to ensure the (joint) agenda stays on point. The account plan does not have to be long and complex; on the contrary, keeping the plan short and pointed at key business issues only helps direct attention to procurement value and increases ease of adoption in the business.

Summary and conclusions

There are several shapes and forms commonly used to organize the procurement function. All these organizational structures have their pros and cons, and a company needs to weigh these in the context of procurement potential and its interest in investing for greater procurement success. Aligning with the business and the board are prerequisites for procurement success. In order for the procurement team to set itself up for success, it is key that it considers roles and responsibilities, cross-functional teaming and account planning with the business as techniques to align with the colleagues it needs to work with and executives it works for.

A final consideration about internal alignment is that this topic is not exclusively relevant to procurement. Professionals in other supply chain functions and even non supply chain functions need to align with peers and leadership just as much to ensure they maximize their business value contributions. As a result, this chapter holds relevance even for those readers that may never end up working in procurement!

03

The strategic procurement cycle

CARLOS MENA

The strategic procurement cycle, introduced in Chapter 1, is a process for developing, delivering, executing and learning from procurement strategy in a continuous improvement process (see Figure 3.1). This iterative process allows organizations and individuals to evaluate and learn from their actions before embarking on a new cycle.

In this chapter, we will go through each stage of the strategic procurement cycle and describe the activities, tools and techniques that can help procurement professionals when going through this process.

The strategic procurement cycle aims to connect and align the overall strategy of the organization and the different business units with day-to-day procurement activities. Each stage of the cycle has its own objectives and outcomes, which are described in Table 3.1.

Articulate procurement's vision, mission and goals

Having a clear vision, mission and goals is vital for the success of practically any endeavour, and strategic procurement is no exception.

FIGURE 3.1 The strategic procurement cycle

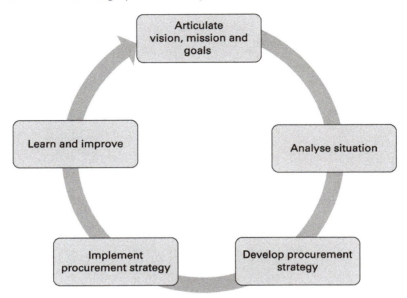

TABLE 3.1 The strategic procurement cycle – objectives and outcomes

Stage	Objectives/outcomes
1. Articulate vision, mission and goals for procurement	To develop the mission, vision and goals of procurement, setting the long-term direction for the function and ensuring alignment with the organization's strategy.
2. Analyse situation	To understand the context in which procurement operates and identify the main trends, potential obstacles and critical success factors.
3. Develop procurement strategy	To create a strategy that can deliver the mission, vision and goals of the function, taking into consideration the resources available and the context in which the organization operates.
4. Implement procurement strategy	To manage the strategy implementation process to ensure the goals are achieved at the right time and cost, and that strategy becomes embedded in the operation.
5. Learn and improve	To evaluate the results of the implementation process and ensure learning is gained and used for the next planning cycle.

However, these three concepts are often abused, so it's important to start with some clear definitions:

- *Vision*: a statement that describes what the organization (or function) wants to be. It's a future-based statement that conveys a sense of long-term aspirations.

- *Mission*: a statement of purpose that defines what the organization is and what it does. It's a present-based statement that communicates why the organization exists.

- *Goals*: goals are specific outcomes sought by an organization or function to pursue its vision and mission. Organizations, and functions within them, generally have multiple goals simultaneously, but it is vital to ensure congruence.

The vision, mission and goals need to be in line with the overall organizational strategy and be supported not only by the procurement function but also by the rest of the organization. For procurement to fulfil this role, it is essential to achieve two forms of alignment. First, alignment with the organization's strategy, which is done by understanding the organization's vision, goals and value propositions, and ensuring that the procurement function can contribute to and, if possible, influence these ambitions. For instance, if the organization is competing on cost, procurement's focus should be on reducing/containing costs. Conversely, if the organization has decided to pursue a differentiation strategy, procurement will need to find ways to support value to the customer while maintaining costs under control.

The second form of alignment is across process, cutting across organizational functions and interorganizational boundaries. Here, we need to understand how we contribute to the goals and strategies of other functions and business units within our organization. This is particularly important in large organizations because different business units might have different ambitions and expectations from procurement. To deliver value for internal customers, we have to understand their needs and put in place the resources to respond to them. This alignment can be facilitated through organizational structures that allow procurement professionals to be closer to their internal customers.

Procurement needs to be involved in the overall strategic planning process for the organization and its business units to achieve both forms of alignment. However, this kind of engagement depends largely on the profile and prominence of the procurement function within the organization. When the procurement function is less mature and has little visibility within the organization, it is necessary to actively engage in conversations, both up the hierarchy and across organizational functions, to ensure we listen to our colleagues and that our voice is heard.

NASA provides an excellent example of mission, vision and goals for its procurement function (see case study). It clearly distinguishes between its future vision (ie acquisition excellence) and current mission (ie optimal business solutions).

CASE STUDY

NASA procurement's vision, mission and strategic goals

Vision

Acquisition excellence in an evolving environment.

Mission

To explore and execute innovative, effective and efficient acquisition of business solutions to optimize capabilities and operations that enable NASA's missions.

Strategic goals

Goal 1: Develop, train, inspire and motivate the acquisition workforce.

Goal 2: Deliver exceptional, timely acquisition of business solutions and results to enable NASA's missions.

Goal 3: Develop sound and flexible procurement processes that integrate the acquisition workforce.

Goal 4: Deliver procurement policy that is required, clear and easily implemented.

SOURCE NASA (2019, 2020)

Having defined the goals of the function, it is vital to identify the key performance indicators (KPIs) that will determine if these goals are achieved or not. One useful tool for this is the balanced scorecard, developed by Kaplan and Norton (1992, 1996). The balanced scorecard helps translate strategy into operations, facilitating the processes of communication, implementation and learning. The balanced nature of the scorecard helps to avoid excessive focus on financial measures, by forcing us to reflect on other dimensions of performance in which procurement can deliver value to the organization and its customers.

The balanced scorecard aims to link the goals of the function with the performance metrics. It does so by focusing on four different perspectives: financial, customer, internal, and learning and growth. Each perspective addresses a specific question about how the organization performs to achieve its goals. Table 3.2 provides some examples of the goals and measures expected under each perspective.

TABLE 3.2   Example of a balanced scorecard for procurement

Financial		Customer/stakeholder	
How do we look to shareholders?		How do customers see us?	
Goals	*Measures*	*Goals*	*Measures*
Efficient procurement Improve procurement's financial contribution	– procurement cost to spend ratio – average purchase order processing cost – cost savings as % of managed spend – cost avoidance as % of managed spend	Internal customer satisfaction Improve time from requisition approval to PO placement	– annual survey of internal customers – average cycle time
Internal processes		**Learning and growth**	
What must we excel at?		How can we continue to improve, create value and innovate?	
Goals	*Measures*	*Goals*	*Measures*
Improve supplier deliveries Improve compliance Agile acquisitions Strengthen partnerships	– on-time, in-full deliveries – quality (PPM) – internal audit compliance – cycle time – partnerships survey – number of active partnerships	Develop procurement professionals and leaders Employee satisfaction Improve knowledge management	– % certification – training spend per employee – survey (% of satisfied employees) – documentation and dissemination of lessons learned

Analyse situation

To develop a robust procurement strategy, it is necessary to have a good understanding of the supply chain for each category and to have performance indicators that allow us to evaluate and track changes in performance. This process requires extensive research to identify the organization's competitive position, its strengths and weaknesses, and its relationships with the supply chain. This needs engagement with current and potential suppliers and other stakeholders who can affect or be affected by procurement operations. Procurement needs to understand the context in which it operates and identify the levers at its disposal to influence organizational performance.

At the top level, we need to analyse the environment to understand the external trends that are likely to influence strategy. This general overview is often done through common management tools such as PESTLE (Political, Economic, Social, Technological, Legal and Environmental), and SWOT (Strengths, Weaknesses, Opportunities and Threats) analysis. A detailed description of these tools is beyond the scope of this book, but, for the interested reader, we recommend a general text on management tools and techniques (eg Armstrong, 2006).

The next level of analysis is conducted at a category level to evaluate the organization's competitive position in the marketplace, assess the balance of power and understand what key factors influence performance. The aim is to understand the current and future relationships with the suppliers. In this section, we review two main approaches to understanding the relationships with the supply base: supply market analysis and spend analysis.

Supply market analysis

A common procurement tool to help understand the balance of power in buyer–supplier relationships is *supply market analysis*. The tool gathers intelligence from market structures and supplier strategies and identifies potential risks and opportunities.

Information required for a supply market analysis can often be gathered from secondary sources. However, some primary data will likely be necessary, particularly in some of the most dynamic and innovative sectors, where secondary data can be outdated or non-existent. It's important to point out that some of the tools used at the environmental analysis stage might provide useful information for the supply market analysis.

This approach is usually applied at a category level, so a first step is to develop *category profiles*. We need to gather data such as commodity descriptions, product classifications, market sizes and general trends. Sources of secondary data here include market research and investment analysis reports, trade journals and conferences. Primary data can be collected directly from current and potential suppliers through site visits and interviews.

To evaluate the *market structure*, we can use the *five forces* model proposed by Michael Porter (Figure 3.2). This tool can be used both to evaluate the forces that shape an industry and assess the balance of power in a business context (Porter, 1979). Porter identifies five important forces that determine the competitive advantage of an

FIGURE 3.2 Porter's five forces model of competition

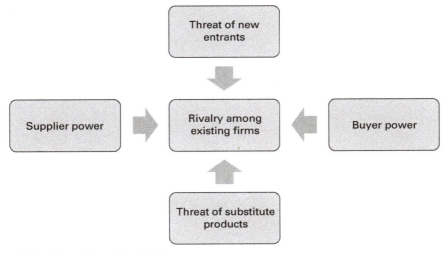

SOURCE Adapted from Porter (1979)

organization: supplier power, buyer power, competitive rivalry, threat of substitution and threat of new entrants. Clearly understanding the balance of power vis-à-vis suppliers is one of procurement's main prerogatives, and it is vital to do it for each key input or category to determine the most appropriate strategy to follow.

Procurement also has a responsibility for keeping an eye on potential new entrants and the emergence of potential substitutes. As a function that is close to the supply market, procurement is in a unique position to pick up signals of potential threats; for example, in situations where there are capacity constraints in the supply market, or in cases where suppliers are trying to move up the chain and become competitors.

Another critical element of supply market analysis is to identify the *key market indicators* for each supply category. Market indicators will depend on your industry and type of commodity, and different kinds of indicators can be relevant to your organization. Some key categories of indicators include:

- *economic indicators*, such as pricing, interest rates and employment;
- *production indicators*, such as production indices per sector and capacity utilization;
- *pricing inflation indicators*, such as the retail price indices (RPI/RPIX), consumer price indices (CPI) and the purchasing managers' indices in different markets.

The analysis of market indicators can help us identify trends for each category, including seasonality and cyclicality of markets, as well as potential shifts in the marketplace that could affect prices or threaten continuity of supply.

Analysing the situation can be a complex and laborious process; however, procurement professionals do not have to carry all this weight on their shoulders. Many of these tools are likely to have been used by the organization to develop its overarching strategy, and procurement should tap into and adapt them to their specific context.

Spend analysis

Critical to understanding the impact of procurement and supply on the organization is *spend analysis* (or *expenditure analysis*), which is essentially an evaluation of all organizational expenditure on goods and services. This analysis tells you how much has been spent on each category, with whom and for which part of the organization. Usually, this is represented as a spend cube, like the one presented in Figure 3.3, where all purchases, both for products and services, are segregated by users, suppliers and categories.

Spend analysis provides vital information for strategic procurement decisions, such as make versus buy, supplier collaboration and partnerships, and category management strategy. Furthermore, the information resulting from spend analysis can also be used as a basis for budgeting and forecasting, and identifying potential opportunities for improvement.

It's important to note that spend analysis should not be based on purchase price alone but instead should aim to reflect the total cost of ownership (TCO). This approach and other tools for strategic cost management are discussed in detail in Chapters 6 and 7.

FIGURE 3.3 Spend cube

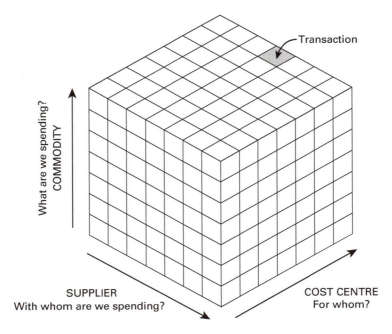

Develop the procurement strategy

The development stage involves producing a strategic plan that will guide the procurement organization to achieve its vision, mission and goals. A procurement strategy should communicate, both internally and externally, what the aspirations and goals of the function are, and how they will be achieved. It specifies the priorities at a category level, the approaches to engage with the supply base, the capabilities required, and the management systems needed to operate and develop these capabilities.

Arguably, the most common tool for developing a procurement strategy is based on the work of Peter Kraljic (1983). Kraljic's matrix classifies product/service categories according to financial impact and supply risk. These terms are used as a proxy for 'how big is the category?/how much money is involved?' and 'how dependent are we?/how much risk exposure is there?'. These two variables are used to create a two-by-two matrix, commonly known as the Kraljic matrix (Figure 3.4), which classifies categories of spend into four types: strategic, bottleneck, leverage and routine.

FIGURE 3.4 The Kraljic matrix

STRATEGIC IMPORTANCE TO PURCHASING	HIGH	LEVERAGE ITEMS • obtained from various suppliers • represent a large share of the product cost • small changes in price have a strong effect on the product **Competitive bidding**	STRATEGIC ITEMS • obtained from one supplier • product for which supply is not guaranteed • represent considerable value **Partnership**
	LOW	ROUTINE ITEMS • usually have a small value per unit • there are many alternative suppliers **Systems contracting**	BOTTLENECK ITEMS • represent relatively limited value in terms of money • vulnerable in regard to their supply **Secure continuity of supply**
		LOW HIGH **COMPLEXITY OF THE MARKET**	

SOURCE Adapted from Kraljic (1983)

The Kraljic matrix suggests that for routine items, with low financial impact and low risk, firms should seek simplicity through systems contracting and other forms of consolidation. For *leverage* items, where supply risk is low but financial impact is high, the strategy is to seek cost efficiencies through approaches like competitive bidding and global sourcing. *Bottleneck* items are interesting because even if they do not have a significant financial impact, they represent a risk to supply. Here the strategy is to secure continuity of supply through supplier diversification, as well as through contractual and relational governance mechanisms. Finally, for *strategic* items, where both financial impact and risk are high, firms should seek close partner-ships with suppliers to secure continuity of supply and garner benefits from collaborative relationships through joint value creation and cost improvement efforts.

The sourcing diamond, or sourcing gemstone, is a tool originally developed by the consultancy Kearney, to refine the strategic direc-tion for each category (Clegg and Montgomery, 2005). The sourcing gemstone (Figure 3.5) is often used in tandem with the Kraljic matrix, as it presents two broad strategic paths for procurement, one focused on exercising power and one on creating mutual advantage.

On the left side of the sourcing gemstone are the strategies intended to exercise power over suppliers: global sourcing, best-price evalua-tion, and volume concentration. These strategies align well with the two low-risk categories in Kraljic's matrix (routine and leverage). On the right side of the gemstone, we have strategies geared towards creating mutual advantage with suppliers: relationship restructuring, joint process improvement, and product specification improvement. These align better with the high-risk categories in Kraljic's matrix (bottleneck and strategic).

The Kraljic matrix and the sourcing gemstone provide insights into the approaches that can be used to extract value from supply markets and help managers decide which procurement strategies to adopt. Nevertheless, it is essential to recognize that financial impact and supply risk are not the only factors that influence procurement deci-sions and that there are alternative models that consider other factors

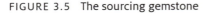
FIGURE 3.5 The sourcing gemstone

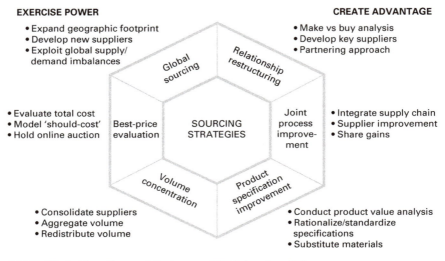

SOURCE Adapted from Clegg and Montgomery (2005); based on AT Kearney

to support procurement strategy formulation (see, for example, Gelderman and van Weele, 2005). In fact, Kearney, the consultancy behind the sourcing gemstone, has proposed a more complex approach called the Purchasing Chessboard®, that outlines 64 different procurement strategies (Schuh *et al*, 2017). However, this approach has been criticized because of its excessive complexity.

To ensure that everybody is engaged with the procurement strategy, it's vital to develop it cooperatively. This can be through workshops, conversations, negotiations and interactions between members of the procurement team and other key internal and external stakeholders. This will lead to a procurement strategy that is shared by the organization and one that is more likely to succeed.

Implement procurement strategy

This stage involves executing the strategy developed in the previous stages. There is no point in carefully crafting a strategy if it is not implemented effectively. However, many organizations admit to not being very good at executing strategy (Neilson *et al*, 2008). This is because strategy implementation tends to be a complex change management process in which we have to win hearts and minds.

Procurement professionals tend to be familiar with traditional project management tools such as work breakdown structures (WBS), Gantt charts and critical path analysis (CPA) (Meredith and Mantel, 2012). These tools can help schedule the project, allocate resources and manage progress, but they tend to focus on the project's tangible and measurable elements, such as time and cost. For strategy implementation to succeed, we also need to deal with the softer, intangible aspects of change management.

A tool that can help us understand the potential barriers to change during strategy implementation is stakeholder analysis. A stakeholder is any individual or organization who can affect or be affected by your organization's operation. Failing to recognize the needs of stakeholders can create obstacles, delay implementation and even damage relationships. Therefore, it is essential to create a stakeholder register in which the potential for both threat and cooperation is identified (Savage *et al*, 1991).

A stakeholder map charts the perceived benefits or threats of a particular strategy for each stakeholder. The map also includes information about each stakeholder's responsibilities, their current level of commitment and the level of commitment required to implement the strategy. This indicates the efforts and actions needed to secure the right level of support. Figure 3.6 presents a simplified example of a stakeholder map.

It is important to note that stakeholder maps should be treated as confidential documents, as some of the stakeholders might not appreciate how the procurement team perceives them.

Neilson *et al* (2008) evaluated why organizations fail to execute strategies and identified four fundamental building blocks that executives could use to influence success in executing strategy:

- *Decision rights*: Having clarity of the responsibility for making decisions and knowing who is accountable for what. This should also provide clarity of boundaries for decision making.
- *Designing information flows*: Information that flows freely and accurately across organizational boundaries. People have access to the information they need when they need it.

FIGURE 3.6 Example of a stakeholder analysis map

Stakeholder	Perceived benefits or threats	Responsibility	Level of commitment					Actions
			Opposed	Indifferent	Compliant	Help it work	Enthusiastic support	
Chief procurement officer (CPO)	Flagship project; reduce costs	A					XO	Seek sponsorships; keep informed
Global sourcing team	Flagship project; hit KPIs	R					XO	Communication, teamwork, performance measurement
Production	Risk of supply, effects on existing supplier	C	X	→		O		Jointly prepare transition and contingency plans
Warehousing	Increased inventory levels; fewer deliveries	C		X →	O			Map impact on budgets and operations. Show benefits
Marketing	Risks for availability and responsiveness	I	X	→		O		Jointly prepare transition and contingency plans
New supplier	New customer, but not major	C				X →	O	Develop relationship. Find opportunities to grow
Existing supplier	Lower volumes; inefficiencies	C	X	→	O			Find incentives; involvement in future opportunities
Finance director	Reduced operating costs; impact on cash	C		X →		O		Demonstrate ROI. Mitigate impact on cash flow

R = Responsible; A = Accountable; C = Consult; I = Inform
X = Perceived current level of commitment
O = Level of commitment required for success
→ = Amount of change needed

- *Motivators*: There are clear objectives and measures of performance, and expectations and progress are communicated. Individuals and departments are rewarded (both financially and non-financially) for what they achieve.

- *Structure*: There should be a match between the strategy and the structure of the organization. For instance, if the strategy is broken down into categories, the structure should also reflect this. Too many layers in the organizational structure can also be a hindrance to implementing strategy.

The stakeholder map can highlight inconsistencies and gaps in these four success factors and help define how to tackle them. It is instrumental in defining clear boundaries for decision making, establishing reporting lines and identifying the potential motivators we need to put in place to bring everybody on board.

Learn and improve

The strategic procurement cycle is an iterative process, and the vision, mission and goals are the central focus of the cycle. At this stage, we measure performance against the goals and targets, and reflect and learn from our experience. There are three key activities in this final stage:

1 Collect evidence and measure performance.

2 Evaluate performance.

3 Embed and communicate learning.

Each activity is briefly described below.

1 Collect evidence and measure performance

We need to collect the evidence for each of the key performance metrics associated with the strategic objectives. This can be done using the balanced scorecard introduced in stage one. By collecting the necessary information under each metric in the scorecard and comparing it with the original targets, we can identify any performance gaps.

It is important to note that the balanced scorecard is only one approach to measuring and managing performance, and any set of KPIs can be used at this stage.

2 Evaluate performance

Performance is usually evaluated at a meeting involving key members of the procurement team and other stakeholders who have been involved in implementing the strategy. At this meeting, participants will reflect upon the strategic goals and the extent to which they have been achieved.

It is vital to identify success and celebrate it. As mentioned earlier, providing rewards for good performance is one of the critical elements of successful strategy execution. However, it's often more challenging to learn from success because we seldom take the opportunity to reflect on how it was achieved. Understanding the factors that have made success possible is essential to reinforce the right behaviour.

In every implementation, there are things that don't go according to plan, and these are clear learning opportunities. For learning to take place, it's necessary to understand what the obstacles were and why we did not manage to overcome them. This is not about finger-pointing, but about exploring what we can do better next time around. Since we are closing the loop at this stage, it's possible to question both the formulation and the implementation of the strategy. This, in turn, should serve as feedback for the procurement team and the organization as a whole.

3 Embed and communicate learning

Finally, we need to embed the learning into the organization and disseminate it among those who can benefit. What we have to ask is who outside our team could benefit from the learning. It is likely that other functions within our organization and even third parties outside our organization can benefit from this evaluation. This might take the form of specific changes to processes, reports, meetings and even personal conversations with stakeholders.

Some organizations have knowledge management processes and software to capture learning from any implementation. While these can be useful, it is more important that we ensure we are reaching all the key stakeholders who can benefit from the learning and that we act upon any learning points identified.

Summary and conclusions

Procurement strategy needs to be aligned both with the organization's strategy and the processes cutting across the organization. In this chapter, we presented a model that describes how a procurement strategy can be formulated, implemented and evaluated to deliver on its promise of being both strategic and influential.

In this chapter, we have discussed the tools and approaches that can help procurement professionals at each stage of the process. Table 3.3 presents a summary of the tools and approaches at each stage.

The approaches and tools described in this chapter indicate what should happen at each stage of the strategy cycle, providing a template for organizations to follow. However, the toolkit is by no means

TABLE 3.3   Tools and approaches for procurement strategy development

Stage	Tools/approaches
1. Articulate mission, vision and goals for procurement	Mission, vision, goals Balanced scorecard
2. Situation analysis	PESTLE, SWOT, supply market analysis, spend analysis
3. Develop procurement strategy	Kraljic's matrix, sourcing gemstone
4. Implement procurement strategy	Project management: WBS, Gantt/PERT charts Change management: stakeholder management
5. Continuous improvement	Performance measurement: balanced scorecard, KPIs Learning: debriefing, reporting and dissemination

comprehensive, and most organizations will have alternative approaches to formulating and delivering strategies. Hence, this general template can and should be modified to fit each organization's context and culture.

References

Armstrong, M (2006) *A Handbook of Management Techniques: A comprehensive guide to achieving managerial excellence & improved decision making*, 3rd edn, Kogan Page, London

Clegg, H and Montgomery, S (2005) 7 Steps for sourcing information products, *Information outlook*, **9** (12), pp 34–9

Gelderman, C J and van Weele, A J (2005) Purchasing portfolio models: a critique and update, *Journal of Supply Chain Management*, **41** (3), pp 19–28

Kaplan, R S and Norton, D (1992) The balanced scorecard: measures that drive performance, *Harvard Business Review*, **70** (1), pp 71–9

Kaplan, R S and Norton, D P (1996) *The Balanced Scorecard: Translating strategy into action*, Harvard Business Review Press, Boston, MA

Kraljic, P (1983) Purchasing must become supply management, *Harvard Business Review*, **61** (5), pp 109–17

Meredith, J R and Mantel, S J (2012) *Project Management: A managerial approach*, Wiley, Hoboken, NJ

NASA (2019) Annual Procurement Report: Fiscal Year 2019, National Aeronautics and Space Administration, https://www.nasa.gov/sites/default/files/atoms/files/annual_procurement_report_2019_final.pdf (archived at https://perma.cc/Z35Y-HP3N)

NASA (2020) About the Office of Procurement, National Aeronautics and Space Administration, https://www.nasa.gov/office/procurement/about (archived at https://perma.cc/6G32-X5V2)

Neilson, G L, Martin, K L and Powers, E (2008) The secrets to successful strategy execution, *Harvard Business Review*, **86** (6), pp 60–70

Porter, M E (1979) How competitive forces shape strategy, *Harvard Business Review*, **57** (2), pp 137–45

Savage, G T, Nix, T W, Whitehead, C J and Blair, J D (1991) Strategies for assessing and managing organizational stakeholders, *Academy of Management Executive*, **5** (2), pp 61–75

Schuh, C, Raudabaugh, J L, Kromoser, R, Strohmer, M F, Triplat, A and Pearce, J (2017) *The Purchasing Chessboard: 64 methods to reduce costs and increase value with suppliers*, 3rd edn, Springer, New York, NY

PART TWO

Procurement and the supply network

04

Supplier relationship management

REMKO VAN HOEK

Supplier relationship management (SRM) is the core procurement process that focuses on everything that happens after the strategic sourcing process. SRM focuses on the programmatic management of ongoing supplier relationships over time. Whereas strategic sourcing ends with a contract, SRM uses that as its starting point. SRM has a longer time horizon than strategic sourcing and is focused on driving continuous improvements jointly with the most important suppliers. In this chapter, the rationale for focusing on supplier relationships is introduced and a basic framework for SRM is offered. Challenges in implementing SRM and new opportunity areas in supplier relationships are discussed.

The structure of this chapter is as follows. The next section discusses why we focus on SRM, after which the framework for SRM (the how) will be introduced. Each step of the framework will be detailed, and a discussion of key challenges in implementing SRM will be offered.

Why focus on supplier relationships?

The strategic sourcing process is the process that leads to the development of relationships with suppliers, negotiated and contracted terms and conditions for the operational ordering process. SRM has everything to do with what happens after the contract is signed and the sourcing process is completed. This contract is used in the ordering cycle to place orders against and work together operationally on a day-to-day basis. For the most important suppliers, companies may choose to develop an ongoing relationship focus and a proactive approach to managing that relationship for continuing value creation. Arguably SRM is the transition from 'money in the sky' in a sourcing strategy to 'money on the table' at the end of a sourcing process and actual 'money in the pocket' or realized benefits in a working relationship.

For procurement, not engaging in SRM leads to the risk of:

- the business thinking procurement only negotiates the deal but is 'missing in action' when something goes wrong, or the contract needs to be executed and implemented;
- contracted savings and benefits 'leaking away' and never being 'cashed';
- suppliers considering procurement less credible because it is not involved in the actual business allocation but only in asking for preferential terms;
- narrowing procurement's scope to negotiations, not doing business together and limiting its focus to the 'deal', not the collaboration.

In addition to avoiding those risks, there are additional benefits of focusing on relationships, as both parties can focus on continuous improvement efforts and openly share challenges and strategies with each other. In turn, this can lead to productivity gains, risk reduction, ongoing savings, and potentially process improvements and innovative opportunities that may go far beyond the initial contract agreed to at the end of the strategic sourcing process.

CASE STUDY

Bayer

Bayer, the Germany-based pharmaceuticals and life sciences company, considers SRM a key process and capability. 'Our top suppliers have a big impact on our business,' says Thomas Udesen, Bayer's CPO, 'we have developed a playbook that we use across categories and suppliers for governing and developing the relationships over time. Benefits include greater productivity and more opportunities to innovate.' The company approaches the relationship with a two-sided approach; both sides need to benefit and invest in the relationship for it to thrive and succeed.

SAME page framework for structuring SRM

Figure 4.1 shows four basic steps involved in implementing SRM:

1 **Select** suppliers to drive relationship efforts.

2 **Align** organizations, contact points and relationship governance.

3 **Measure** performance with a scorecard exchange.

4 **Exchange** improvement opportunities and efforts.

FIGURE 4.1   SAME page framework

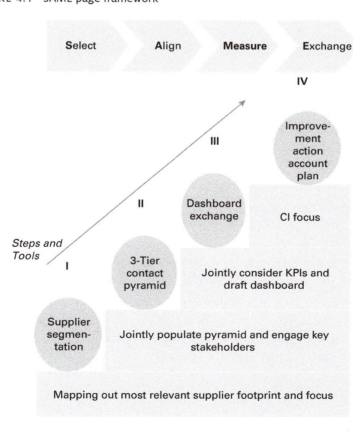

Select: segmenting the supply base

Key to SRM is the reality that the resource intensity and the exclusiveness of collaboration means there are only a few suppliers with whom true collaboration can be established. Not only because of demands on the supplier and because of limited capacity on the procurement side but also because the majority of suppliers will be preferred or contracted suppliers at best.

There are many approaches to supplier segmentation, but organizations often rely on Kraljic's matrix, discussed in Chapter 3. In the strategic segment, there is a financial relevance and a risk need to drive for long-term and close relationships, while the routine segment does not warrant a lot of attention and hands-on involvement; little risk and small financial benefit to be had. The leverage segment is the segment in which good-old negotiations and driving competitiveness in the market is the default approach; there are multiple suppliers and little risk of switching while there is a sizeable financial impact. Bottleneck suppliers may be smaller in financial impact but critical for supply; focus here will be on ensuring supply rather than driving financial benefits. Key to supplier segmentation is to focus most resources and efforts on key suppliers and less on others – it is very much a prioritization scheme, just like any customer segmentation is.

In that spirit, what Figure 4.2 introduces as sails of the windmill is the customer segmentation that a supplier might use, and it contrasts these with the procurement segmentation to explore what position procurement finds itself in. For example, being seen as a strategic customer by a strategic supplier (far top right) introduces a good match and opportunity to develop a long-term partnership. If, however, a supplier you consider strategic sees you as a customer that needs to be streamlined, for example not a very attractive account where they do not want to focus too many resources, you are in a risky position with that supplier. The approach here might be to seek and attract competitors. Equally so, if on the top left, you see suppliers as leverage and you are looking at them to drive competition. In contrast, suppliers see you as a strategic account, and you are in a good position as they will not likely turn you away and will work very hard in a competitive setting.

FIGURE 4.2 Supplier segmentation windmill

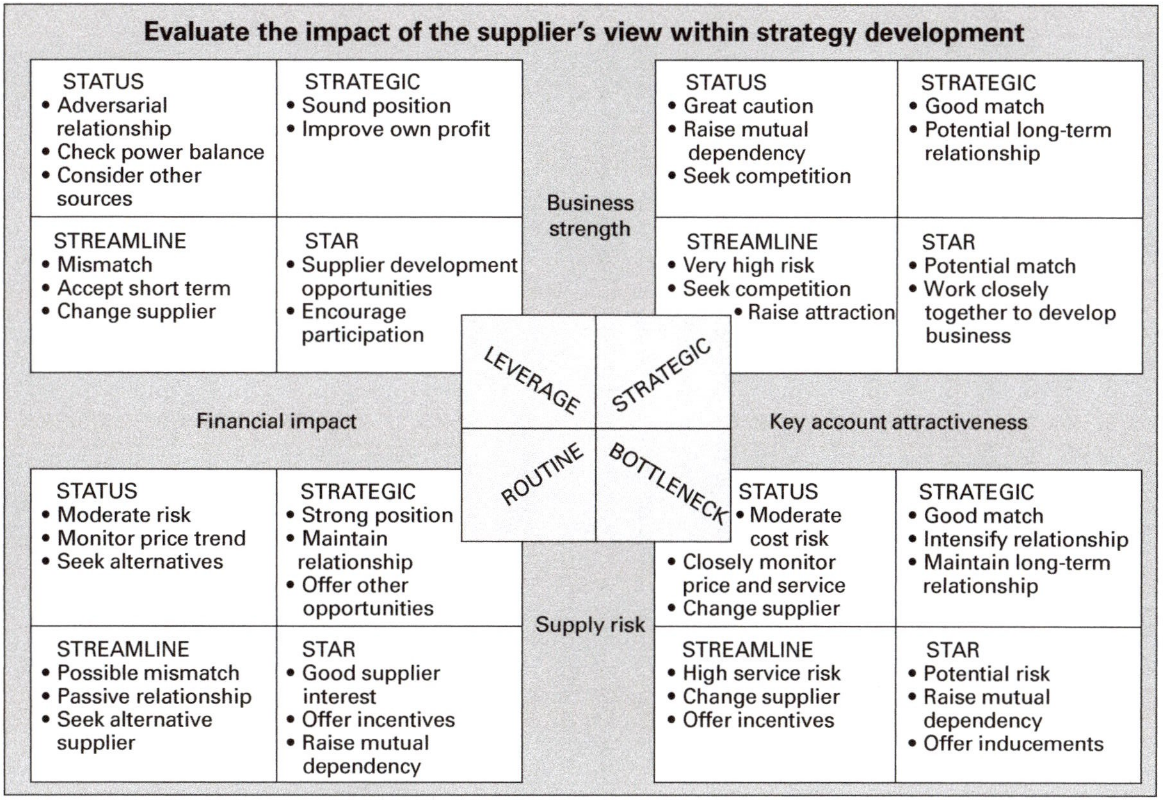

Evaluate the impact of the supplier's view within strategy development

	LEVERAGE	STRATEGIC
	ROUTINE	BOTTLENECK

Axes: **Business strength**, **Key account attractiveness**, **Financial impact**, **Supply risk**

STATUS
• Adversarial relationship
• Check power balance
• Consider other sources

STRATEGIC
• Sound position
• Improve own profit

STREAMLINE
• Mismatch
• Accept short term
• Change supplier

STAR
• Supplier development opportunities
• Encourage participation

STRATEGIC
• Good match
• Potential long-term relationship

STATUS
• Great caution
• Raise mutual dependency
• Seek competition

STAR
• Potential match
• Work closely together to develop business

STREAMLINE
• Very high risk
• Seek competition
• Raise attraction

STATUS
• Moderate risk
• Monitor price trend
• Seek alternatives

STRATEGIC
• Strong position
• Maintain relationship
• Offer other opportunities

STREAMLINE
• Possible mismatch
• Passive relationship
• Seek alternative supplier

STAR
• Good supplier interest
• Offer incentives
• Raise mutual dependency

STRATEGIC
• Good match
• Intensify relationship
• Maintain long-term relationship

STATUS
• Moderate cost risk
• Closely monitor price and service
• Change supplier

STAR
• Potential risk
• Raise mutual dependency
• Offer inducements

STREAMLINE
• High service risk
• Change supplier
• Offer incentives

SOURCE Based on Purspective

Align: contact pyramid

Some strategic and well-embedded suppliers have many connections with their customer organization on multiple levels and in multiple business areas. Key to streamlining relationship efforts is to leverage on these connections and to provide structure, sponsorship and ownership to the engagement. Typically the two sides of the relationship will specify operational, relationship and sponsorship levels of contacts, in which the operational interactions can be day to day and about normal business transactions. The relationship level interaction may be on a business period by business period time frame involving relationship and account management from both sides. And the top level could be bringing together senior leaders, who sponsor and oversee the relationship, less frequently.

Measure: supplier dashboard

A supplier dashboard is used to measure and track suppliers' performance in the eyes of users in the business and against the agreements reached with procurement. As such, it is very much a barometer of progress and performance and a basis for discussion about improvement opportunities.

Rules of thumb for good dashboards include:

- Do not overcomplicate the metrics and the size of the dashboard; this just burdens the supplier without contributing to the main purpose of the dashboard.
- The most important role of the dashboard is to serve as a basis for discussion.
- The dashboard should be two-sided to truly reflect the relationship.
- Focus KPIs on improvement areas and relationship priorities and do so consistently over time.

- Inform KPIs with supplier selection criteria and sourcing strategy to avoid inconsistency across procurement processes (eg, we select on different criteria than we evaluate on).

In addition to driving discussion about improvement opportunities, dashboards can be used to:

- showcase progress and joint wins;
- engage business leaders and stakeholders in the relationship in a nuanced way (not biased by the most recent interactions);
- create a road map for the relationship in the periods to come;
- allocate business volumes based upon progress and relative performance;
- inform updates and adjustments to sourcing strategies.

Exchange: improvement plans

Joint investment and innovation efforts represent a hallmark of achievement in SRM – this is when the two organizations really connect and engage deeply together. Improvement actions may initially be focused on more operational areas in the early days of the relationship. Over time they move to new areas of collaboration and investments identified at the relationship level and sponsors at the top level of the relationship pyramid.

Suppliers may also become collaborators in risk management. It is feasible to discuss risk drivers and levers in the relationship and the supply chain, and to jointly develop scenarios and mitigation approaches to reduce and respond to risks. Risk metrics may become part of the scorecard, and supplier and buyer can team up to monitor for possible risks, including supply disruptions, quality issues or logistics challenges. In Chapter 8, we will further develop the theme of risk management.

Challenges in implementing SRM

There are several critical challenges in implementing SRM, which help explain why many procurement executives plan to and would like to be more active in SRM than they are today. These challenges are:

- It is hard to make the case for devoting time and resources in SRM against the track record of savings from focusing on sourcing.

- Engaging the business in SRM is critical yet can be difficult to structure in a sustainable manner.

- Doing SRM well requires a different skill set for procurement staff than traditional procurement and strategic sourcing.

Making the case

Many procurement organizations justify investment (in procurement leaders, team development and technologies) and the need for the business to engage with procurement based upon the financial benefits of strategic sourcing. Simply put, procurement can be self-funding with the savings it can generate, provided business alignment and sufficient calibre and capacity of staff. While sourcing leads to the contracting of (better) terms and commercial conditions, SRM is about bringing in those contracted returns during the usage period of those contracts. Arguably this takes more time and is a more ongoing effort. Yet pitching for the resources to do so can be challenging; most of the measurable benefits have already been claimed in a business case for sourcing. Yet without SRM, these benefits might never be capitalized upon.

Additionally, it is difficult to turn the economic benefits of having relationship managers into hard cash, such as negotiated savings. Yet the business might have come to expect hard ROI from procurement on the back of its strategic sourcing track record. On top of that, business leaders and peers will have multiple connections with suppliers already in place. This might lead them to challenge the need for procurement to involve itself in those relationships.

Some strong arguments that procurement leaders use in favour of SRM include:

- avoid benefits leak past the contracting stage, for example seeing the agreement through;

- risk and dependence on critical suppliers justify resources and ongoing commitment;

- there are many things you cannot put in the contract, such as premium access to supplier resources and innovations;

- increased credibility and reliability as a customer of choice with suppliers.

Gaining business support and participation

Just as in strategic sourcing, business engagement is a critical success factor in SRM. Populating the relationship and governance pyramid with business contacts is critical to enable a close tie to operations, users and budget holders. It enables a real-life SRM conversation and makes the path to actioning outcomes shorter. However, when requesting business participation in an SRM programme, business leaders often push back using the argument that they already have supplier connections and conversations, and can get the supplier in the room if there is an issue.

While this is true, experience shows that procurement can add some things to this connection, including:

- Coherent processes, calendars, governance structures and dashboards to provide consistency and rhythm to the conversations that otherwise are often infrequent, informal and not tied to improvement actions.

- Clear roles and responsibilities in relationship management and the opportunity to deliver bad messages that business leaders often like to stay away from to 'keep the relationship intact'.

- An enterprise perspective to the relationship rather than the (by definition) partial view of individual business leaders.

Different behaviours and skill sets

Managing relationships is different from negotiating terms and conditions. Needless to say, the ability to effectively implement SRM is critically dependent on adding to the skill set of the procurement department. Procurement managers and buyers have traditionally played hard-ball. Their job has been to secure better deals from suppliers. But what if suppliers are a gateway to innovation, quality and sustainability? And what if old-school procurement practices are standing in the way of tapping into the wisdom of suppliers?

SRM requires three key things:

1 Centring supplier engagement around customer market opportunities, stewarding supplier contributions 'front of the house' to new revenue and market differentiation rather than just focusing upstream on the supplier deal only.

2 Being transparent about where we need help from suppliers, where there are new business opportunities and facilitating access to users in the organization, as opposed to creating speed bumps to existing spend in the negotiations process.

3 Broadening the definition of success to include multiple elements of value, rather than just a narrow focus on price, and actively selling and marketing this story.

Three examples help illustrate this change:

- Vodafone, the telecommunications multinational, takes supplier relations all the way into its marketing to consumers. The company has focused supplier relationships and engagements around the voice of its customers. It awards suppliers annually for their contribution to innovating new market propositions. A recent advertising campaign featured a supplier-developed service feature that transfers information from one mobile phone to the next while in the store as a reason for switching to Vodafone. The focus of procurement has moved from the back of the supply chain to 'front of house'.

- P&G offers an excellent example of openness in buyer behaviour, and recently published its procurement sustainability scorecard in an effort to articulate where it seeks and needs supplier help. In the process, the company created transparency into what procurement's objectives are, where it stands today and where it's heading – obviously a break with the old tactic of blowing smoke into a negotiations process to gain the upper hand.

- Unilever invites suppliers into innovation summits. At these events, procurement provides opportunities for suppliers to pitch innovations to business and R&D leaders. Procurement also markets the event and stewards suppliers with the Unilever board, leading to most board members attending the events and sponsoring projects.

These examples show how SRM is less about traditional buying that focuses upstream on deals, reduces transparency and introduces speed bumps to create leverage for price-driven negotiations. Instead, it is about focusing on customer value and moving from the back of the house to the front room. It is about being transparent about where help is needed, moving from playing poker to showing your cards.

As the case study from Mars shows, part of the key change is to start listening to suppliers, measuring their feedback and addressing this consistently, to capture negotiated benefits and drive for premium access. This is an obvious shift from traditional strategic sourcing behaviour focused on telling suppliers what it takes to qualify and negotiating them into procurement's mould.

CASE STUDY
Mars Europe takes the voice of the supplier

Voice of the customer exercises are common in marketing and sales organizations; to learn how you are seen as a supplier and where and how you can work together better is normal practice. As a result, suppliers often know better than procurement how well they are doing, and procurement can often learn a lot from what suppliers are hearing across the business.

Perhaps the approach of Mars Europe to start measuring and tracking the voice of the supplier is particularly good practice. It addresses the need to listen and learn, and be open and engaged with suppliers as a basis for having a meaningful relationship.

Mars Europe has a philosophy, captured in Figure 4.3. It drives for supplier engagement by being connected, focused on reciprocity in the collaboration (as opposed to one-sided, looking after its own benefits only), integrity in their business dealings, clarity in regular and open discussions, and simplicity in interorganizational processes. It also measures how it performs against these goals using a very simple survey (which is intentionally simple) with 10 questions that map against these five objectives.

Mars uses the Gallup Supplier Engagement framework, and Gallup administers and neutrally processes the data by business unit and at the individual category level. This is reported as a 'heatmap' that compares scores per objective and by area of spend, part of the world and procurement team. In this way, improvement opportunities can be spotted and made very personal and focused.

The findings, good or bad, are discussed with participating suppliers to show that they are taken seriously and to drive a discussion about how to improve and collaborate better moving forward. Over time this consistent focus from the Mars Europe team has really started to change the interactions for the better and started helping Mars Europe move into a different type of relationship with its suppliers.

FIGURE 4.3   Mars Europe philosophy

* Know what Mars expects
* Regular, open and honest discussions

Clarity

* Can't imagine our business without Mars
* Mars takes risks

Connectivity

* Eager to hear best practice ideas
* Both need each other

Reciprocity

Supplier Engagement

* Easy to do business with
* Easy to deliver excellence

Simplicity

Integrity

* Count on each other
* Problems, mutually satisfactory resolution

CLARITY	Q01	My company knows exactly what Mars expects from us.
	Q02	My company has regular open and honest discussions with Mars about their needs and expectations.
SIMPLICITY	Q03	Mars is always easy to do business with.
	Q04	Mars' processes and procedures make it easy for my company to deliver excellence.
INTEGRITY	Q05	My company and Mars can always count on each other to do what we say we will do.
	Q06	When problems occur, Mars works with my company to resolve them in a way that is fair to both of us.
RECIPROCITY	Q07	When we share our best practices or new developments with Mars, they are eager to hear our ideas.
	Q08	We both need each other in order to be successful.
CONNECTIVITY	Q09	We can't imagine our business without Mars.
	Q10	Mars takes risks to help my business succeed.

Sparks the Conversation

'It is good to discuss not only based on core performance indicators, but in something that is commonly shared between the two of us'
Raw Materials Buyer, Food

Keeps the Book Open

'This allowed us to keep in contact with a supplier that lost the last tender. At the end they helped us out when the new supplier was unable to deliver the service, even decreasing the prices according to their best offer'
Sourcing Operations Manager, Petcare

Allows a Benchmark

'We use SE10 as a metric to track the impact of a new forecast accuracy project, that way we can measure success based on the same scale used to identify the problem'
Sourcing Coordinator, Drinks

Raises Awareness

'This tool gives Commercial a stronger voice within the business'
Strategic Sourcing Manager, Petcare

Making the change

While SRM is often talked about, one of the keys to future success in procurement will be to address challenges and consider the steps identified in this chapter so far. To assist in planning and plotting the change, Figure 4.4 offers a possible change programme for implementing SRM.

The top five horizontal bars in the diagram represent areas that need to change in order to implement SRM:

- business centric for it to succeed and be of sufficient value;
- supported by changes in metrics;
- enabled by tools;
- impacting people in the procurement team to change the ways of working;
- focused on engaging suppliers differently.

From a change management perspective, suggestions are offered in the bottom two horizontal bars. The statements on the far right of the figure illustrate how stakeholders should be thinking about an SRM programme for the change aspects to be positioned well in the areas listed. These can serve as a litmus test: 'Are we thinking and talking about this programme in the right way?'

The vertical bars represent the four likely stages in the development and roll-out of an SRM programme. They start with *pitching* the programme by articulating SRM in business benefits, engaging the procurement team and testing receptiveness of a few suppliers for such a programme. In the *preparation* stage, the toolkit is developed or rounded out as a basis for the programme, including the design of governance pyramids with the business, and scorecards. Profiles of roles in the programme are developed to enable a change in ways of working, and the selection of suppliers to pilot the programme with is finalized. The *pilot* can contain 10–15 suppliers to collaborate with to put the tools into action and test it, to show early wins and identify areas of improvement. In the *propel* stage, these can then be rolled out to a larger group of suppliers over time, and a customer of choice status can be targeted.

FIGURE 4.4   Change programme design for implementing SRM

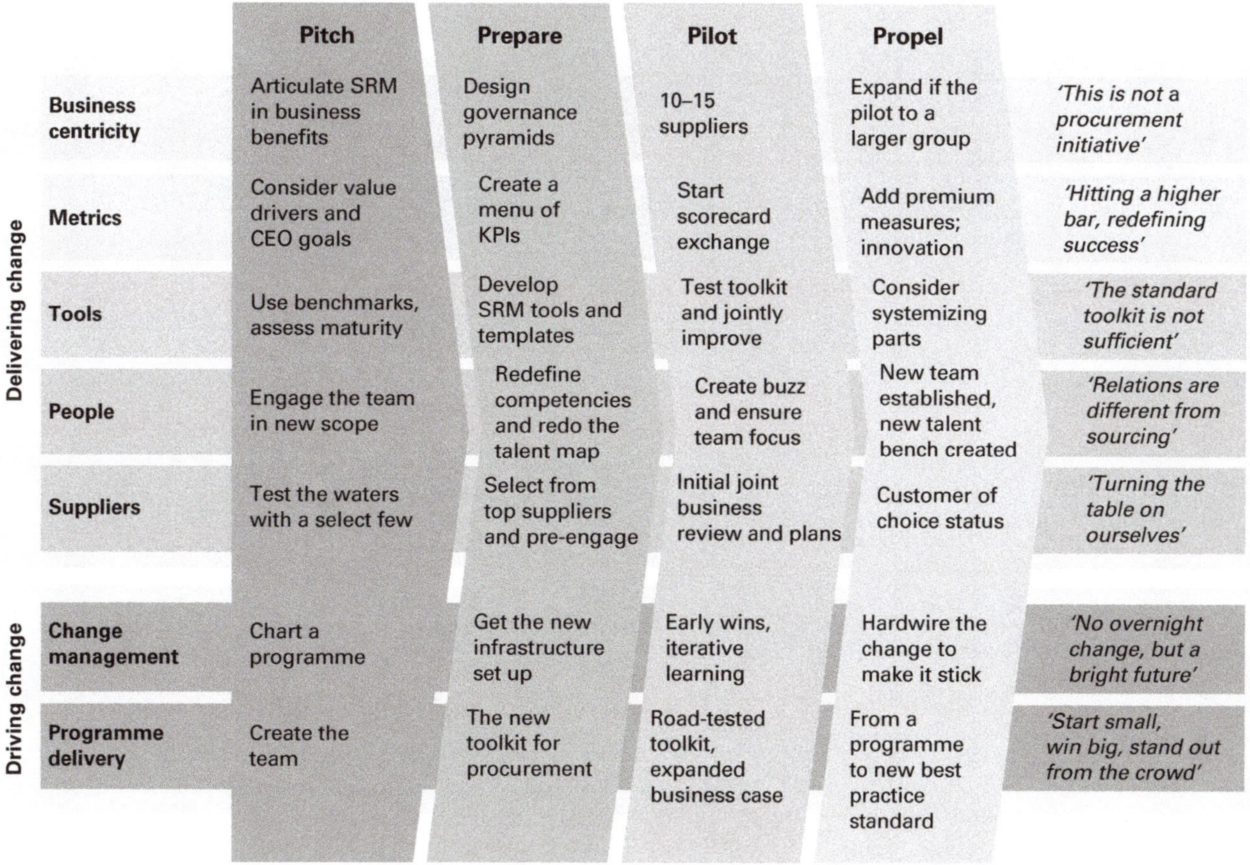

	Pitch	Prepare	Pilot	Propel	
Business centricity	Articulate SRM in business benefits	Design governance pyramids	10–15 suppliers	Expand if the pilot to a larger group	'This is not a procurement initiative'
Metrics	Consider value drivers and CEO goals	Create a menu of KPIs	Start scorecard exchange	Add premium measures; innovation	'Hitting a higher bar, redefining success'
Tools	Use benchmarks, assess maturity	Develop SRM tools and templates	Test toolkit and jointly improve	Consider systemizing parts	'The standard toolkit is not sufficient'
People	Engage the team in new scope	Redefine competencies and redo the talent map	Create buzz and ensure team focus	New team established, new talent bench created	'Relations are different from sourcing'
Suppliers	Test the waters with a select few	Select from top suppliers and pre-engage	Initial joint business review and plans	Customer of choice status	'Turning the table on ourselves'
Change management	Chart a programme	Get the new infrastructure set up	Early wins, iterative learning	Hardwire the change to make it stick	'No overnight change, but a bright future'
Programme delivery	Create the team	The new toolkit for procurement	Road-tested toolkit, expanded business case	From a programme to new best practice standard	'Start small, win big, stand out from the crowd'

Delivering change — Business centricity, Metrics, Tools, People, Suppliers

Driving change — Change management, Programme delivery

Barriers to implementing SRM: where are we today?

Based on a survey conducted by the Cranfield School of Management and PwC, Figure 4.5 shows average scores across respondents for potential barriers. Respondents were asked to grade the potential barriers (the items listed vertically) on a scale ranging from –3 (not an issue at all) to +3 (a major barrier). The figure shows rank-ordered average scores for the items.

Figure 4.5 implies that there is major work to do to implement SRM to its potential, beginning with the basics. Lack of team capacity, the highest-scoring item, says as much: 'we do not have the time on our hands to do this'. Arguably that is a bit defensive and tactical – maybe SRM is not 'another thing to do' but a way to work differently. Perhaps many procurement departments are still busy with sourcing and not yet ready for SRM (recall the Chapter 2 procurement sub-processes and the point that SRM tends to come into main focus after strategic sourcing on the way to procurement maturity).

The second item refers to the fact that procurement is still seen as a cost saver and lacks integration with business processes. This reinforces the need to align the definition of success, not just in words but also in the perception and understanding of stakeholders. This links back to the need to improve internal alignment and make the case that procurement has a role to play in relationships, both internally and externally. The lack of a procurement toolkit appears as the third issue, which also links to the gap in capabilities. We hope that in this chapter we have started to address this issue by suggesting some practical approaches to developing an SRM programme.

The other items link back to the top three issues; of course, current conversations with suppliers are more operational in focus if we do not have the team bandwidth and tools to change the conversation and put an SRM programme in place. And no wonder that suppliers are not fully engaged in SRM efforts, nor are these embedded in an existing business process.

FIGURE 4.5 Barriers to SRM: average importance scores ranging from −3 to +3

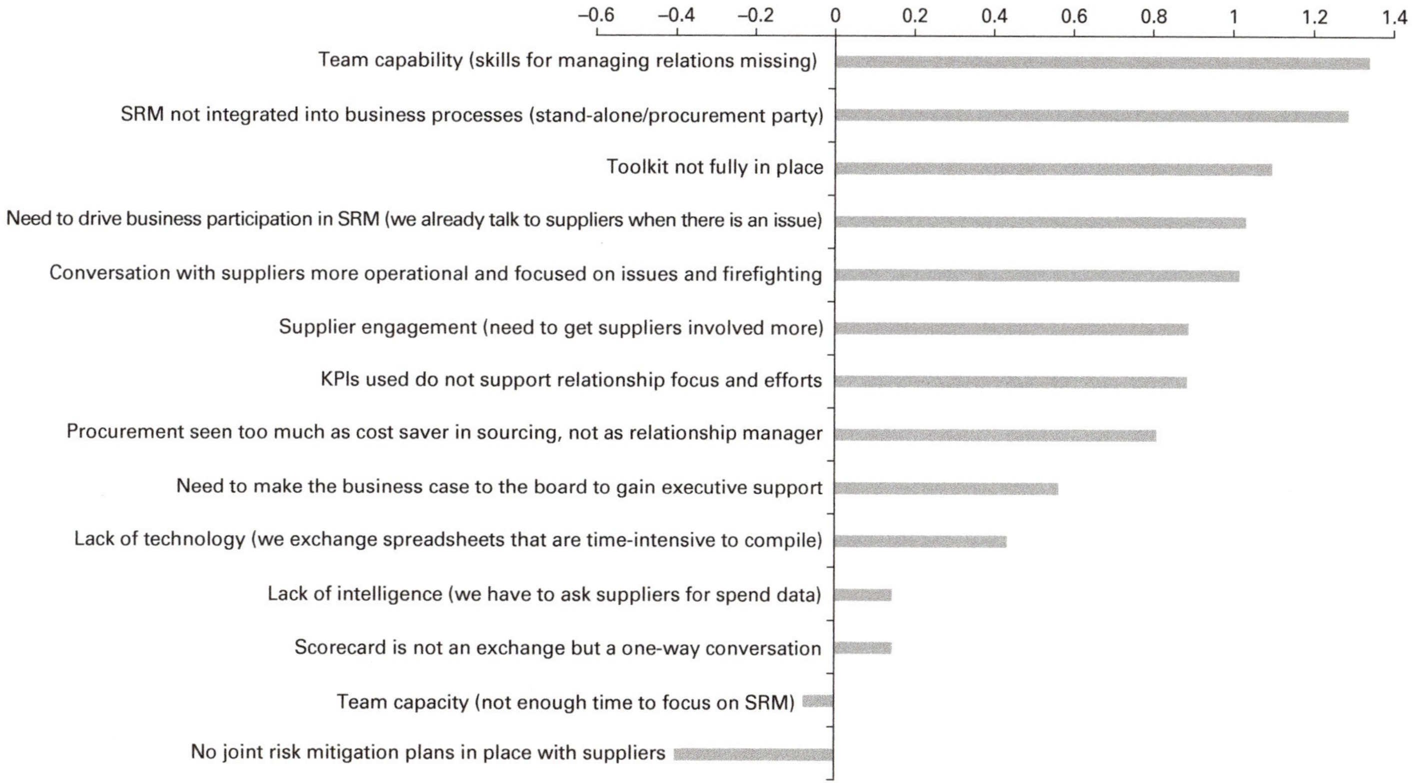

Summary and conclusions

Supplier relationship management is gaining focus and attention in strategic procurement, and this makes sense. SRM helps avoid negotiated benefits leaking away; it helps companies get to continuous improvement opportunities and ensures procurement can help see through a negotiated result. Key elements of implementing SRM are: 1) segmenting suppliers and selecting key relationships to invest in; 2) establishing a contact pyramid to align contacts between the two firms; 3) establishing a dashboard to measure performance; and 4) engaging in improvement planning on an ongoing basis. Barriers to change to be cleared for successful SRM include the need to make the case for SRM, gaining business support and engagement in the supplier relationships, and changing skills and behaviours of procurement teams.

With the 'SAME page framework' in place, the business engaged and the team capabilities developed, procurement puts itself in a perfect position to broaden its impact and expand the value it adds to the company and the supply chain. In reality, this will be easier said than done, and today SRM is talked about more than it is practised. Yet the path forward is clear – supplier relations and the active engagement of procurement in them is the gateway to bigger value and business benefits.

05

Global sourcing

MARTIN CHRISTOPHER

While trade between nations has been a feature of economic activity for thousands of years, it is only in the relatively recent past that we have seen the dramatic rise in what is now termed 'global sourcing'.

For centuries the norm for most industrial organizations was to source materials and components close to the point of manufacture or assembly. This is a business model that we might term 'local-for-local'. Thus, a motor car assembled in, say, the UK in the 1950s would likely have been built from component parts made in the UK. However, in the latter part of the 20th century, there was a dramatic rise in the manufacturing capabilities of what have come to be called 'low-cost countries' where wage costs, in particular, were significantly less than wages in the traditional manufacturing locations. The attraction of sourcing in countries where the cost of labour was low was further enhanced by the revolution in global shipping driven by the move to containerization. This as much as anything enabled the disadvantage of distance to be overcome as the cost of moving products around the world was dramatically reduced, at least in real terms.

A further factor accelerating the trend to offshore sourcing was the reduction in trade barriers, which previously had served to make the transfer of products across borders artificially expensive through tariffs, quotas and other trade restraints. A classic example of the liberalization of cross-border trade was the creation of the European Economic Community (EEC) – now the European Union – or 'Common Market' in 1957. What was originally a trading community of six countries had by 2013 been enlarged to a group of 28 nations with others applying to join. The formation and enlargement of the Common Market meant that for the first time it was possible to move materials, components or finished products across country boundaries within the single market economically and efficiently. Thus began a move away from 'local-for-local' solutions to a more regional manufacturing and sourcing strategy. Other similar trading agreements have since been created in different geographies, for example NAFTA in North America, MERCOSUR in South America and ASEAN in Asia Pacific. On a wider global stage, the trend to increased cross-border trading has been given further lubrication by the actions of bodies such as the World Trade Organization (WTO), whose aim is to remove barriers to international trade wherever possible.

The end result of these seismic shifts in the global business environment was that by the start of the 21st century, global sourcing had become the norm for many companies. In some cases, whole industries had been displaced from their traditional bases to locations on the other side of the planet.

As noted earlier, many companies have sought to lower their costs of goods sold by moving production or sourcing to countries where the costs of doing business are lower. A key driver for this decision was the considerable difference in the cost of labour between Western countries and many Asian locations. As a result, in the closing decades of the 20th century, low-cost country sourcing became a dominant trend across most industrial sectors.

However, in an increasing number of manufacturing processes the proportion of costs accounted for by direct labour has declined significantly in recent decades. Higher wages in countries once considered cheap places to manufacture have narrowed the gap between the West and the emerging economies. In addition, automation, robotics and new manufacturing technology have radically changed the cost equation for many businesses, further calling into question the need to source from these locations.

CASE STUDY
The shift to low-cost countries in the fashion industry

The European fashion and textile industry provides an example of the impact that the shift to low-cost country sourcing has had on an entire industrial sector. Western Europe until recently was the world's biggest exporter of textiles and was a leader in the production and export of clothing and footwear. Italy in particular was a significant manufacturer of textiles, clothing and footwear. However, in recent decades much of that manufacturing has moved offshore with a consequent impact on the economy both nationally and locally. One example of this shift to global sourcing is the case of Benetton. Only 20 years ago, 90 per cent of its clothes were made in Italy; now that figure is nearer to 10 per cent. The Benetton example is typical of what has happened across the entire Italian textile, clothing and footwear industry. Employment levels in these sectors have fallen dramatically as the trend to global sourcing has accelerated. The same scenario has been repeated across these sectors in the rest of Western Europe.

The anti-globalization movement

Recently a number of voices have been heard questioning globalization in general and free trade in particular. While there have always been those who believe that globalization is potentially harmful to established domestic industries and the employment that they provide, the generally held view has been that trade between nations is, in aggregate, beneficial. However, partly perhaps as a result of populist political movements, there is an emerging demand from some quarters for a greater emphasis on generating more jobs in the home economy. In the United States, for example, following the 2016 presidential election, pressure has been placed on corporations to reduce their dependence on offshore sourcing and manufacturing and to reverse the trend towards greater globalization.

More recently, trade disputes between the United States and China have added to the uncertainty about future sourcing arrangements. Coupled with the disruptions to global trade caused by the COVID-19 pandemic, the effect has been that many companies are now questioning the sustainability of offshore sourcing generally.

However, even the likelihood of 're-shoring' happening on any scale is low, if only because local supply sources and capabilities may no longer exist. Nevertheless, procurement professionals need to be aware that their sourcing decisions will increasingly be placed under a public spotlight, and they will need to be able to justify their actions, not just from a narrow corporate viewpoint but from a wider economic and social perspective.

Further pressure is also coming from the need for organizations to be able to demonstrate that their supply chains are ethical and sustainable. There is an increased concern today among consumers, employees and other stakeholders for greater transparency to ensure that the provenance of all products and materials can be accounted for. In many countries, legislation has been introduced requiring companies to audit their supply arrangements. The risk of non-compliance is likely to be greater when supply chains become extended as a result of global sourcing because of reduced visibility beyond the first-tier suppliers. Hence the need for the highest levels of due diligence before a sourcing decision is made.

The true costs of global sourcing

While global sourcing is still widespread across most industry sectors, there is an emerging point of view that suggests that in some cases, the decision to move offshore might not always be the best strategy. Indeed, it can be argued that the dynamics of the global business environment have altered the supply chain landscape sufficiently to justify a re-evaluation of the global sourcing decision. There is some evidence that many companies have decided to move offshore without a full analysis of all the costs involved. A study by Cranfield School of Management (Christopher *et al*, 2007, 2011), based on an extensive review of a cross-section of British industry, found that in the majority of cases these decisions had been taken using a very narrow definition of cost. Typically, the report found, companies were heavily influenced by the lower factory gate price that could be achieved through low-cost country sourcing and did not account for the true total end-to-end supply chain costs.

Ideally all sourcing decisions should be subjected to a rigorous 'total cost of ownership' analysis. In other words, all the costs, both visible and hidden, should be taken into account to determine the appropriate sourcing strategy.

What are these costs? Among the most important are the following:

- *Factory gate price*: This is the obvious starting point for the analysis. It refers to the unit cost per item and should reflect not only the purchase price but also any additional local costs such as taxes, insurance and other periodic expenses.

- *Inventory costs*: The longer the delivery lead time, the greater will be the inventory in the pipeline. Also, more safety stock will probably be required to buffer against the variability in both demand and supply. This inventory has to be financed and will also impact cash flow.

- *Transport costs*: Clearly, shipping product greater distances will incur higher transport costs. Global shipping rates are often quite volatile, and so what might look like a relatively low rate today may not be in a few years' time. In some instances, expediting costs may be incurred if emergency airfreight has to be used.

- *Risk costs*: The potential hidden costs of global sourcing include the impact of such factors as: currency exchange rate fluctuations; geopolitical risk leading to potential supply disruptions; the chance of stock-outs if demand is greater than anticipated; obsolescence or mark-down costs if demand is less than expected; the risk of loss of intellectual property, etc.

- *Other costs*: Often it is not always recognized that managing extended supply chains brings with it significant additional costs. Quality is often difficult to control, and firefighting and problem-solving may be more difficult at a distance. Insurance costs for goods in transit may be higher, and there will be customs clearance costs and possibly duties/tariffs to be paid.

Because global sourcing usually implies a longer supply chain, at least in terms of 'end-to-end' lead times, there can also be significant working capital implications attached to the global sourcing decision. One of the key business performance metrics to be impacted by longer lead times is the *cash-to-cash cycle time*.

Cash-to-cash (C2C) cycle time is a useful measure of the length of a company's immediate supply chain. C2C reflects the elapsed time from the point when cash is spent with suppliers until cash is received from customers. Figure 5.1 shows how it is calculated.

Where surface shipping is involved, the end-to-end pipeline time will often be measured in months rather than weeks. As a result, the inventory in the pipeline will inevitably increase. First, because the transit time is longer, the cycle stock will increase proportionately. Second, because of the likelihood of greater variability in lead times, the more the safety stock will be needed to buffer the uncertainty. The increased inventory has to be financed and, in addition, there will be cash flow implications from the extended C2C cycle time, which could have critical implications for the financial health of the business.

Shifting centres of gravity

All supply chains have a 'centre of gravity', which is determined by the combined effects of the 'pull' of various forces on the demand side and the supply side of the firm. The resultant centre of gravity impacts many supply chain decisions, including sourcing strategy. Figure 5.2 suggests that a number of important issues need to be weighed in the balance when supply chain design and sourcing decisions are taken.

FIGURE 5.1 Cash-to-cash cycle

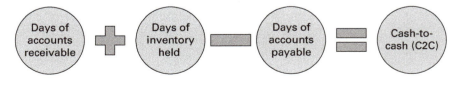

FIGURE 5.2 Changing centre of gravity

The supply chain's centre of gravity is shifting

Supply-side vectors

Demand-side vectors

- Labour costs
- Materials and resource availability
- Skills
- Transport costs

Centre of gravity

- Changing demographics
- Disposable income
- Changing consumer preferences
- Industry development

On the demand side the forces or vectors that will impact the centre of gravity include:

- *Changing demographics*: As a result of population growth dynamics and changing age profiles, some markets globally are growing more rapidly while others are shrinking. For example, Unilever now reports that over half its turnover comes from developing countries.

- *Differences in disposable income*: A major change is taking place regarding the relative growth in spending power in different countries. Traditional markets in the West, which once dominated global spending, are now being overtaken by the emerging economies in terms of expenditure.

- *Changing consumer preferences*: As populations transition from being predominately rural towards increasingly urban and as their disposable income rises, so too does the pattern of consumption change. The massive growth in the demand for cars in China and India provides a good example of this, as do the changes in diet now occurring in many emerging economies with a consequent rise in the demand for dairy and meat products.

- *Industry development*: The major shift in industrial production away from Western economies to low-cost countries has had a major impact on trade flows and the level of demand for raw materials. Serving these fast-growing markets while still needing to maintain a presence in static or declining markets is a challenge many companies face today.

Similarly on the supply side, a number of factors will act as counter-vailing forces impacting the centre of gravity. These include:

- *Labour costs*: Many sourcing decisions in recent decades have been motivated by the desire to take advantage of lower labour costs. So-called 'low-cost country sourcing' has been based on the desire to improve competitiveness by manufacturing or sourcing in locations where labour costs are a fraction of those in more traditional locations. However, what were once significant differentials in labour costs have often been eroded through wage inflation. Likewise, new potential contenders for the description of low-cost countries have emerged.

- *Material and resource availability*: Inevitably the availability and cost of key input materials and resources such as metals, energy, chemicals and other commodities are a major influence on sourcing decisions. With rising demand and, in some cases, declining supply, the availability and prices of these critical input factors can be dramatically affected. There is a growing realization among some established manufacturing companies that they will have to reassess their current supply chain arrangements as the economics that prevailed in the past may no longer apply.

- *Skills*: As industries continue to become more knowledge-intensive and dependent upon specific skills and capabilities, access to them becomes ever-more critical. Even in times of high unemployment, companies in many sectors find that they face skills shortages, for example information technology specialists, software designers and engineers. Whereas once it was the Western world that predominated in the supply of these skills, this is rapidly changing as the levels of education and training in the newly emerging economies accelerates.

- *Transport costs*: The cost of moving products across the globe has been highly volatile in recent years. Fuel prices, shipping rates and air freight costs have risen sharply on occasion but have also fallen significantly at other times. This volatility is difficult to factor into sourcing strategy, and hence there is always the possibility that a decision based upon today's cost of transport may be less than optimal at some future point in time.

The implications of shifting centres of gravity in the supply chain for sourcing strategy are significant. In particular, these shifts strengthen the argument for moving supply closer to demand. Most of the thinking of recent decades has been towards centralization of manufacturing and the consolidation of inventories in fewer distribution centres. Now perhaps the economics will increasingly point to sourcing solutions based upon the strategy that, wherever possible, local markets should be served from sources better able to meet their specific requirements – and that could mean a return to the traditional concept of 'local-for-local'.

Moving supply closer to demand

For years the prevailing logic underpinning many business decisions has been the idea of 'economies of scale' and focus. The concept of economies of scale is based upon the principle that when products are made or bought in volume, then the unit cost will be lower because the fixed costs of manufacturing and/or procurement are spread over a greater number of items. Flowing from this concept is the view that if products can be produced in or sourced from dedicated facilities, then the ensuing efficiencies will bring further cost reductions.

This thinking has led many companies to centralize manufacturing in fewer but bigger facilities and/or to source from just a few suppliers to support their (often global) operations. As a result of implementing these strategies, costs may well be reduced, but lead times from order to delivery will probably be longer and flexibility will almost certainly be reduced.

The problem here is that in today's highly competitive marketplace, there is a real need to be faster to respond to changing customer requirements, and so those companies with extended global supply chains may find that they are less able to compete in these dynamic markets.

In response to this challenge, there is an emerging view that perhaps rather than centralized and focused operations, the future may lie in a more 'distributed' supply chain architecture. This is the idea that, wherever possible, supply should be brought closer to demand so that lead times can be reduced and flexibility increased. New manufacturing technology is transforming companies' ability to produce to individual customer requirements in smaller quantities at lower cost. Additive manufacturing, or 3D printing, is an example of how new technology is challenging the conventional wisdom of the economies of scale and focus, as reflected in the case of GE below.

CASE STUDY

GE's 'local-for-local' strategy

GE, one of the world's biggest engineering and manufacturing businesses, has a declared strategy of bringing supply closer to demand. Whereas previously the company had tended to centralize production and serve multiple global markets from specialized facilities, the intention now is to seek out opportunities to build and source products closer to the markets where they will be sold. In a speech in 2016 the then CEO, Jeffrey Immelt, said: 'We will localize. In the future, sustainable growth will require a local capability inside a global footprint. GE has 420 factories around the world, giving us tremendous flexibility. For example, we used to have one site to make locomotives, now we have multiple global sites that give us market access.'

This new strategy reflects the reality of today's marketplace, where the ability to move quickly in response to changing customer requirements can become a major source of competitive advantage.

The impact of global sourcing on agility

A prevailing feature of many markets today is the continuing increase in what some have termed 'clockspeed' (Fine, 1998). What this means is that demand patterns change more quickly than in the past, product life cycles are shorter, and time to market has to become ever faster. We are in the era of 'time-based competition', which places a premium on agility, that is, the ability to respond rapidly to unexpected changes in demand.

There are many prerequisites for agility, but one critical requirement is short replenishment lead times. If demand suddenly changes – either in volume terms or in the mix of products – how quickly can the company respond? It is therefore something of a paradox that just as businesses are embracing just-in-time practices and seeking to become more responsive to time-sensitive customers, they have also often lengthened lead times as a result of global sourcing strategies.

One way to overcome this paradox and to gain the benefits of global sourcing without incurring a loss of responsiveness is by using the principle of *postponement*.

The idea behind postponement is that the final assembly, configuration or finishing of the product is delayed until the shape of actual demand is known. Often that late-stage, postponed activity will take place locally, close to the source of demand. The aim is to keep the product generic for as long as possible. If appropriate, the generic (or 'vanilla') product can be sourced in a low-cost country and then held locally as strategic inventory until the precise customer requirement is known. The point in the supply chain where this strategic inventory is located is often termed the 'decoupling point'.

A good example of postponement is provided by Zara, the world's biggest clothing manufacturer and retailer. Zara often purchases the fabric that it uses for its products in advance from low-cost sources. That fabric is held as strategic inventory in an undyed and unfinished state. Only when local demand has been determined will the cloth be dyed, finished and cut prior to the garment being assembled. This strategy has helped Zara maintain a very high level of agility while keeping total cost and supply chain risk low.

The need for flexibility and adaptability

While agility is clearly a requirement in markets where demand is uncertain and difficult to predict, it may not by itself be sufficient to enable companies to respond rapidly to a fundamental shift in the supply chain's centre of gravity. As was previously highlighted, because of the much more turbulent and volatile business environment that prevails today, these centres of gravity are likely to change more frequently requiring a much higher level of *adaptability* by the supply chain than was the case before.

Because of this uncertainty and rapid change, it is difficult for any organization to predict what future sourcing requirements might be. As a result, it is important not to get locked in to supply arrangements today that might restrict the company's ability to adapt to tomorrow's changed environment. Ideally, when seeking partners in the supply chain the company should adopt an approach to sourcing whereby rather than committing to long-term arrangements that may offer lower prices but constrain future flexibility, the aim should be to look for short-term but very close partnerships. The guiding principle should be that the best sourcing decisions are those decisions that keep the most options open. There will usually be a price to be paid for these options, but that price should be seen as an investment in supply chain flexibility.

Clearly this is a point of view that might not gain a lot of support in companies that have traditionally been inclined to favour solutions that are deemed to be the lowest cost. Putting a value on flexibility is not easy, but actually lack of flexibility when circumstances change rapidly and unexpectedly can be far more costly in the end. The case of Apple is interesting; as the case study below highlights, they have been prepared to invest in longer-term arrangements with key suppliers where they believe those suppliers to be strategically important – the view being that in a volatile and fast-changing market, it can be a source of competitive advantage to control what could be potential bottlenecks in the supply chain.

CASE STUDY

Apple's supply-side strategy

Apple's ability to introduce iconic and innovative products that attract huge consumer uptake is widely recognized. While much of their success is undoubtedly down to the cutting-edge design and functionality of their products, underpinning everything they do is a carefully designed and executed sourcing strategy.

Much of Apple's sourcing is in the Far East, but they have developed extremely close connectivity with their key suppliers to ensure that the highest level of supply chain agility can be achieved. When operating in fast-changing markets where the rate of new product introduction is high and time-to-market critical, the ability to ramp up and ramp down production and shipments is vital. Apple has long recognized this requirement and has achieved a high degree of supply chain agility through a number of strategies.

One key element of their approach to ensuring upstream agility is to enter into long-term contracts with the suppliers of key components, for example for high-resolution retina displays. These contracts are worth billions of dollars and ensure commitment and continuity from those suppliers.

In some cases, Apple negotiates exclusivity arrangements with suppliers, effectively locking out competitors. In other cases, Apple will invest in dedicated precision machinery and equipment on behalf of their manufacturing partners to cement that exclusivity.

Obviously Apple's size gives them some advantage in negotiating supplier agreements, but their willingness to invest in their suppliers and their desire for continuity is a key part of this strategy. In effect, Apple is seeking to ensure that they have access to capacity whenever they need it and in particular to be able to control any potential bottlenecks in their supply chain.

Making the global sourcing decision

After several decades of dramatic growth in offshore sourcing, there are now signs of a more considered approach being adopted by an increasing number of companies. There is a recognition that global sourcing can be the appropriate strategy to adopt in certain circumstances. Equally, however, there will be other conditions when a more 'local-for-local' or perhaps a regional sourcing strategy is required.

The case of the UK textile industry (see case study) highlights what may become a growing trend as more companies start to reassess their offshore sourcing strategy.

CASE STUDY

The UK textile industry – a homecoming?

In the 19th century and throughout much of the 20th century, the textile industry in the UK was a dominant sector across the whole economy and a world leader in terms of the volume of production. However, by the start of the 21st century, the industry was a shadow of its former self, employing less than 100,000 people (compared to well over a million at its height). While this decline was long term over many years, it accelerated towards the end of the 20th century as more and more companies sought to lower costs through moving manufacturing and sourcing to locations that then were considered to be 'low-cost labour countries'.

In recent years however, there have been signs that this trend has slowed and may even be reversing. Companies like Laxtons – a Yorkshire-based manufacturer of a wide range of yarns and fabrics, established for over 100 years – decided in the early years of this century that all their manufacturing activity should be brought back to the UK. The motivation for this decision was that when the real costs of the end-to-end supply chain were recognized – including quality control and delivery lead times to customers, for example, and the need for a more responsive capability – it was clear that manufacturing in the UK made more sense. In addition, the importance of the 'Made in Britain' label was growing as the demand for quality products in the apparel market continues to increase.

This trend to local sourcing in this sector is increasingly being influenced by the growing importance of the 'fast fashion' market. Retailers seeking to compete in this market need suppliers who can respond rapidly and flexibly to trends. Even though the costs of manufacturing and sourcing may still be lower in many countries than in the UK, this cost disadvantage is increasingly outweighed by the marketing advantage that comes from greater agility.

What are the issues that should be taken into account when considering which products or materials to source globally and which to source locally or regionally?

- *How time-sensitive is the market?* A feature of many markets today is that they are increasingly time-sensitive. This is equally true in both business-to-business markets and consumer markets.

Many companies have adopted just-in-time practices and are very dependent on the speed and reliability of inbound supplies. In many consumer markets too, customers expect high levels of availability. In addition, product life cycles are getting shorter in many industries as the pace of technology change quickens or as fashions move on. If time is a critical element in gaining competitive advantage, then global sourcing may not be appropriate if it leads to the lengthening of replenishment lead times and the potential loss of reliability.

- *How stable is demand for the product?* Stable demand implies predictability, and thus the risk of global sourcing in these conditions is reduced. Conversely, if demand is highly volatile and hence less predictable, then the need for agility in the supply chain is clearly greater. Agility, as was previously defined, implies the capability to respond rapidly to unpredictable changes in demand – something that might not be possible if inbound lead times become extended as a result of global sourcing. Hence stability and predictability of demand should be a critical factor in determining the source of supply.

- *What proportion of the cost of goods sold (COGS) is accounted for by labour costs?* As we observed earlier, one of the main factors influencing many companies' decisions to source offshore has been the access to low-cost manufacturing – which generally implies low-cost labour. A key issue, therefore, is the percentage of the cost of goods sold (COGS) for the product in question that is accounted for by labour costs. If the labour content is high then the case for low-cost country sourcing is clearly strengthened. Conversely, if the labour element in COGS is low, then the case is weakened – particularly as labour rates in many so-called low-cost countries continue to rise. Furthermore, given the trend to automation in so many industries, it is likely that the labour content for many products will reduce over time.

- *How transport intensive are your imported materials/products?* One important metric to weigh in the balance when considering global sourcing is the 'transport intensity', that is, what proportion of total landed cost is accounted for by transport? The density of the product is a critical determinant of transport intensity. Density is a reflection of the volume and weight of an item. Products that occupy less space in a shipping container, for example, will be less transport intensive than more bulky items. Given the concern over carbon footprints, this should be an important consideration.

- *What is the value/density of the material/products?* The previous point highlighted the effect of density on transport intensity. A related issue is the value of the product compared to its density. The value/density of a product can significantly impact the financial case for global sourcing since the higher the value and the greater the density, the less important transport costs are relative to total costs. To take two extreme examples: diamonds and cornflakes. Diamonds are high value and very dense, cornflakes are at the other end of the spectrum. Thus both the sourcing decision – assuming of course that there is a choice – and the mode of transport used will be heavily influenced by value/density considerations.

- *Are there any risks to intellectual property?* Intellectual property (IP) concerns the proprietary technology, knowledge, patents, etc, that enable a company to differentiate itself from its competitors. One concern is that if production is moved offshore, there could be a risk that some of that IP might be lost. This is a sensitive area, but it is often suggested that in certain countries the risk of loss of IP is greater than in others. One factor influencing this is the local and regulatory frameworks of different countries. To combat this risk while still taking advantage of low-cost country sourcing, some companies have decoupled their supply chains and source the basic generic product offshore but do the final finishing/configuration – which may involve the application of the more valuable IP – in more secure locations.

- *How transparent is the upstream supply chain?* One of the problems facing many companies if they source overseas is the potential loss of upstream visibility. In other words, they may not be aware of the supply arrangements of their suppliers. Thus while a company might have confidence in the capabilities of their immediate (Tier 1) supplier, they may not have visibility into the second- or third-tier suppliers. Often the biggest risk to the supply chain can lie upstream of the Tier 1 supplier. Those companies that have invested in tools such as 'track and trace' and 'event management' systems that issue alerts if there are deviations from the plan, will be better able to monitor upstream performance and hence feel more confident in offshore sourcing.

Managing a global sourcing network

Given that the decision to source offshore has been taken – hopefully taking into account all of the issues described above – there are some guiding principles and practices that ideally should be adopted. In no particular order the key areas for management action include:

- *Establish an 'end-to-end' process team*: Because global sourcing by definition impacts supply chain performance, it is critical that an 'end-to-end' management approach is adopted for the whole procure-to-delivery process. Rather than relying on the existing business functions to take responsibility for fragmented elements of the supply chain, a cross-functional process team should be tasked with managing the entire flow from the factory to the customer. Supporting the team – which will likely be a 'virtual' team given the global scope of the supply chain – will be an information system that will enable visibility across the extended enterprise. This information system will provide a 'track and trace' capability as well as issuing alerts when there are deviations of performance in terms of 'plan versus actual'.

- *Invest in local management*: Many companies have experienced considerable problems with the implementation of offshore sourcing strategies because of a failure to recognize the importance of a high level of local engagement with those offshore suppliers. It is a mistake to assume that once the sourcing decision has been taken and all the usual due diligence investigations completed that the supplier can be left to get on with it. Instead, local managers should be employed to represent the interests of the business and to ensure that on-the-ground issues that could impact the smooth running of the supply chain are dealt with as they arise.

- *Move to 'factory gate pricing'*: In many cases, companies – particularly retailers – sourcing overseas have negotiated terms of trade based on the principle of paying for the goods on a 'delivered duty paid' (DDP) basis. In other words, they pay the supplier an agreed price based on the supplier absorbing all the costs up to the point of delivery at the final destination. This may be simple to administer, but in effect it can mean that the purchaser may have little control over the supply chain and that major opportunities for cost reduction through freight consolidation are being lost. When individual suppliers are making independent decisions on shipping, then the likelihood is that there will be a lack of transparency of freight costs and that the customer's visibility of the supply chain will be obscured. Instead, the purchasing company should take control of the supply chain by negotiating terms based on the price at the factory gate.

- *Establish a total cost-of-ownership monitoring process*: One of the key tasks of the 'end-to-end' management team, as defined earlier, is to monitor the true total costs of offshore purchasing decisions. Because the business environment is constantly changing, what were thought to be the costs of ownership when the sourcing decision was taken may no longer be the case. The problem for many businesses, as was earlier suggested, is that they do not have the means to conduct this type of analysis. In these situations, it will be necessary to put in place a process to monitor all the costs that are involved from when a replenishment order is placed for an item until when the goods are delivered at their final destination. In addition, all the market costs associated with delayed deliveries, obsolescence, mark-downs, etc, must be accounted for.

- *Build a supply chain 'control tower'*: By their very nature, global supply chains are subject to a greater number of potentially disruptive influences. Longer lead times, as we have seen, can lead to greater levels of variability in delivery lead times. Equally, loss of visibility upstream in the supply chain – particularly at second-tier levels and beyond – can hide potential problems. Companies who can establish a 'bird's eye' view of the end-to-end supply chain and monitor what is actually happening in as close to real time as possible will gain a great advantage. Building the control tower requires the development of a monitoring system, using appropriate metrics, to identify variations from plan and to establish the causes of those variations. The control tower concept will enable the application of 'Six Sigma' methodologies to control supply chain process variation.

Summary and conclusions

Many companies are now reviewing global sourcing decisions that were often made some years ago when the balance of costs and benefits may have been different to those prevailing today. Using a more detailed cost schedule and factoring in issues such as the impact on responsiveness and agility, these companies are concluding that in some instances there is a strong case to be made for reconsidering those earlier decisions.

One thing is certain and that is that a more flexible and segmented approach to global sourcing is required. Thus, rather than adopting a 'one size fits all' approach, a more differentiated strategy should be adopted – sourcing globally when it makes sense and sourcing locally when it does not.

References

Christopher, M, Jia, F, Khan, O, Mena, C, Palmer, A and Sandberg, E (2007) *Global Sourcing and Logistics*, Department for Transport (DfT), Logistics Policy project number LP 0507

Christopher, M, Mena, C, Khan, O and Yurt, O (2011) Approaches to managing global sourcing risk, *Supply Chain Management*, 16 (2) pp 67–81

Fine, C H (1998) *Clockspeed: Winning industry control in the age of temporary advantage*, Perseus Books, Reading, MA

PART THREE

Delivering performance in procurement

06

Strategic cost management

Strategic cost management is not a new idea, but it is an idea that many organizations have difficulty implementing in practice. The concept of strategic cost management is the 'application of cost management techniques so that they simultaneously improve the strategic position of a firm and reduce costs' (Cooper and Slagmulder, 1998). As discussed in Chapter 1, the procurement organization in most companies spends more money than any other area, around 50 per cent of revenue for manufacturing firms, and over 20 per cent for most service firms. As a result, procurement is under constant pressure to reduce costs. Ultimately, companies really want to reduce the types of costs that are wasteful. Reducing such non-value-added costs ultimately improves the organization's profitability because it cuts expenses without reducing revenue.

However, there are different ways to reduce costs. Costs can be reduced in such a way that it actually reduces the value that the organization is delivering to its customers and hurts the organization's competitiveness. It defeats the purpose of cost reduction, which is generally to enhance profitability. Costs can be reduced in such a way that the impact is transparent or neutral to the customer, and it has no impact on the customers' perception of the organization's value. Third, costs can be reduced in such a way that the organization's value to the customer is actually enhanced. The third is the preferred situation and the embodiment of strategic cost management.

The purpose of this chapter is to help the reader gain an understanding of the nature and application of strategic cost management. After introducing the concept of strategically managing costs, this chapter explores three topics in strategic cost management: total cost of ownership/acquisition, cost analysis and kaizen costing.

How to manage costs strategically

The first step to managing costs strategically is to understand the organization's strategic focus. In the case of a for-profit organization or a competitive situation for a non-profit, the question that must be answered is: how does the organization compete to win and retain customers? In other words, how does the organization add distinctive value? There may be different answers to that question by business unit or customer segment. It is important that the procurement organization understands these different competitive strategies among the businesses it supports, so it makes the right decisions to support each business's definition of success. In the case of non-profit or public agencies that are not competitive in nature, but that have the goal of supporting a specific mission, it is essential that they deeply understand the mission and the desired customer deliverables. Whether procurement is buying promotional materials, supplies or items that directly serve the customer, it must be done in a manner that is consistent with the organization's mission and vision. There are three key elements of strategic cost management:

1 value proposition analysis;

2 supply chain analysis;

3 cost driver analysis.

Each of these is presented in more depth below.

Value proposition analysis

Strategic cost management should always begin with understanding the value proposition, because everything that the organization does should support the value proposition, which is sometimes referred to as a unique selling proposition. Value proposition analysis essentially considers how your organization competes within the marketplace. What is it that attracts customers to you to do business rather than to another potential supplier? What advantage do you have to offer your customers above the competition? In order to effectively act upon this, you must understand and speak strategy. This is the only way you can effectively communicate with top management *and* make the right decisions to support the organization. There are some generic strategies that you might be familiar with. These include:

- cost leadership, or being the low-cost provider;
- innovation – doing things first;
- niche – meeting the needs of a specific customer segment.

The three approaches above are classic approaches popularized by Michael Porter (1985) in his classic book *Competitive Advantage*. These approaches to competition are still valid today. However, there are many new approaches as well. The most popular among these include competing based on:

- *Time, or speed to market*: This was a very popular strategy in the late 1990s and continues to be an important approach to doing business today.
- *Service/solution provider*: This has become one of the key ways for organizations to compete in this decade. Being a full-service solution provider requires a high level of understanding of customer needs and flexibility in willingness to meet those customer needs.

CASE STUDY
IBM's transformation to solution provider

IBM is an example of a company that transformed itself from an innovative provider of computer hardware and PCs to an innovative, full-service solution provider of IT systems, service, consulting and support, aimed at solving its customers' problems. Its mission states: 'IBM attracts and retains some of the world's most talented people to help solve problems and provide an edge for businesses, governments and non-profits. Innovation is at the core of IBM's strategy. The company develops and sells software and systems hardware and a broad range of infrastructure, cloud and consulting services' (IBM, 2013). By 2017, IBM had revised and expanded its mission statement, noting its emphasis on being a solution provider, not a seller of systems and services as in 2013. IBM's mission is 'to lead in the creation, development and manufacture of the industry's most advanced information technologies, including computer systems, software, networking systems, storage devices and microelectronics. And our worldwide network of IBM solutions and services professionals translates these advanced technologies into business value for our customers. We translate these advanced technologies into value for our customers through our professional solutions, services and consulting businesses worldwide.' This remains as IBM's mission in 2021 (Mission Statement.com, 2021).

As illustrated by IBM, organizations may use a combination of the above strategies. In addition, the strategies used may change over time, and vary by product and business unit. Early in its 100-plus-year history, IBM sold commercial scales and cheese slicers as well as tabulators (IBM, 2013). Thus, one of the important things for procurement to be aware of is the current strategy for the products/services that it supports. This understanding facilitates making the correct buying decisions to support that strategy. For example, if you are not aware of the strategy of your organization in selling its new product or service line, you will have no way of gauging how to weigh supplier selection criteria such as quality, price and supplier technical innovation. Without this knowledge and understanding of your organization's strategy, you could make the wrong decision and actually undermine the long-term success of the product. With the value proposition in mind, procurement is in a position to begin to analyse ways to enhance the value proposition, while reducing cost.

Supply chain analysis

Supply chain management is defined as the management of the flow of information, inventory, cash and processes from the earliest supplier to the ultimate consumer, including the final disposition process. This definition embodies a broad process perspective of the supply chain. Thus, analysing the supply chain must take a broad perspective, because of the many interrelationships and interactions among members of the supply chain.

Why has there been such an increased focus on supply chain management? Supply chains took on a new focus during the global COVID-19 pandemic of 2020–21. It became clear that excellent and agile supply chains were essential to preventing disruption, and to recovering quickly from large surges in demand, shortages, and reduced supply of labour and other inputs. Further, supply chain costs are often the major percentage of an organization's total costs. With companies relying heavily on suppliers for so much of their added value, it is more important than ever to select the right suppliers and manage them effectively. Poor supply chain performance increases costs as an organization attempts to recover from its mistakes. It can also create customer ill-will, which could have customers looking for alternatives. With the rapidly changing competitive environment organizations face today, the ability to design the right supply chain and continuously redesign it as needed can keep the organization agile and ahead of the competitive curve.

CASE STUDY
Amazon's supply chain redesign

An example of an organization that has continually redesigned its supply chain to stay ahead of the curve is Amazon. Amazon was founded in 1994 and began business as an online seller of rare and difficult to locate books in 1995, with no inventory or warehouses, shipping out of a garage (Hartmans, 2021). When it discovered that it was difficult to be profitable doing this and wanted to reach a larger audience, it broadened its product line to all types of books and began to build distribution centres in order to better serve its customers.

Amazon's stated mission is: 'We seek to be Earth's most customer-centric company. We are guided by four principles: customer obsession rather than competitor focus, passion for invention, commitment to operational excellence, and long-term thinking' (Amazon, 2021). To support this mission, in the early 2000s it launched many other product lines, including electronics, CD, DVD and video sales, home, computer, kitchen and toy stores (Office Timeline, 2020). Amazon has continued to adapt its supply chain, adding product lines, distribution centre locations and the newest technology to serve its customers more fully and more rapidly. It went on a warehouse-building spree, investing $13.9 billion to build 50 new distribution centres in a two-year period beginning in 2010, and can have a distribution centre operational in 10 months (Kucera, 2013). It spent $775 million in 2012 on Kiva robots to improve distribution centre accuracy and speed (McCorvey, 2013). In 2017, it spent around $200 million on a single warehouse in Utah that employs only 180 workers, but many robots (Coombs, 2017). It is currently investing heavily in transportation to provide its own delivery services, including Amazon Air (Berman, 2021).

Cost driver analysis

Cost driver analysis relates to what processes, activities and decisions actually create costs in a supply chain. The cost drivers vary over time, and among different products and services. Some of the generic cost drivers include:

- Use of nonstandard materials and components and parts.
- Lengthy approval processes.
- Scale of operations. For example, a very large manufacturing operation, retailer or distributor must have high volumes in order to be profitable. A smaller operation may actually be unprofitable at high volume levels because of overtime costs, inefficiency in operations, and machine breakdowns and maintenance issues.
- A high level of finished goods product mix. The more options the organization offers its customers, the more inventory it may have to carry, and the more flexible it must be in its production operations.

Cost drivers can also be related to the organization's internal and external processes. One of the key issues to remember is that cost drivers are not inherently good or bad. They must be analysed relative to their value. For example, a high level of finished goods product mix clearly adds complexity and cost relative to offering a single product. However, that might be the organization's value proposition: to provide customers with a higher level of product offerings than the competition. Thus, one must always look at cost drivers relative to the value that they add and how these cost drivers are related to other costs.

Returning to the Amazon example, Amazon made a clear decision to invest heavily in its fulfilment centres and transportation, adding costs to its supply chain. For example, its combined shipping and fulfilment costs grew from $5.5 billion in 2010 (16 per cent of sales) to $78.1 billion in 2019 (27.5 per cent of sales). In explanation of this trend, Amazon notes in each of its 2010–20 annual reports, 'We expect our cost of shipping to continue to increase to the extent our customers accept and use our shipping offers at an increasing rate…We seek to mitigate costs of shipping over time in part through achieving higher sales volumes, optimizing our fulfilment network, negotiating better terms with our suppliers, and achieving better operating efficiencies. We believe that offering low prices to our customers is fundamental to our future success, and one way we offer lower prices is through shipping offers' (Amazon, 2020: 26).

In other words, Amazon is telling its shareholders that it is fully aware that shipping is a cost driver, but it is designing its supply chain to mitigate that, and it believes that its fast and flexible shipping is a key value proposition to its customers! It is counting on the capability of its new distribution centres to add enough customer value at a lower cost per unit shipped to more than pay for its enhanced customer value proposition of increased fast delivery. Given Amazon's strong revenue, profit and market share growth, this investment appears to be working. The benefits of a strategic cost management approach may not come overnight but may represent a long-term commitment to reduced cost and customer value enhancement.

Summary of strategic cost management

Strategic cost management is a way of thinking about how to enhance the customer value proposition while simultaneously reducing cost. Strategic cost management should be part of new product and service design, so that the most cost-effective, highest-value products and services are introduced in the marketplace. Strategic cost management can be incorporated into new product design through target costing, embracing specific cost goals and customer attributes as presented below. Strategic cost management should be part of everyday business operations and support continuous improvement efforts as the external environment, including competition and customer demands, evolves. Most importantly, for strategic cost management to be truly effective, it should be part of the organization's philosophy—a process and a way of thinking that is embraced by everyone, at all levels of the organization. One of the tools to support strategic cost management is total cost of ownership analysis, which entails really understanding the cost of a particular good or service.

Total cost of acquisition/ownership

Total cost of ownership is defined here as a philosophy for understanding all relevant supply-chain-related costs of doing business with a particular supplier for a particular good/service, or the cost of a process or particular supply chain design. In its broadest sense, total cost of ownership looks at the 'big' picture, considering many costs beyond price. When you make strategic decisions, you really want to understand the costs involved, and perhaps even set some targets for what you're willing to pay.

A five-step process to implementing TCO

The five steps to implementing a TCO approach in the organization are as follows:

1 Determine desired benefits of TCO.
2 Form a team to work on TCO analysis.

3 Identify relevant costs and gather data.

4 Fine-tune the TCO analysis, including sensitivity analysis.

5 Present recommendations to top management.

From a strategic cost management approach, TCO is a misnomer, in that TCO must also consider revenue implications. In situations where organizations make a change that is not revenue neutral, it is not enough to simply capture the costs of change; the revenue impact must also be captured. The first step in TCO analysis is deciding why the organization wants to conduct a TCO analysis.

Step 1: Determine desired benefits of TCO

The first step in a TCO analysis is deciding what benefits you are seeking in conducting the analysis. You probably already have a particular project in mind. There may be multiple reasons to conduct a TCO analysis. A list of potential reasons is shown below:

- provide performance measurement;
- framework for cost analysis;
- benchmark performance;
- more informed decision making;
- communication of cost issues, internally and with suppliers;
- encourage cross-functional interaction;
- support external teams with suppliers;
- better insight/understanding of cost drivers;
- build a business case;
- support an outsourcing analysis;
- support continuous improvement;
- help identify cost savings opportunities;
- prioritize/focus time on high potential opportunities.

The benefits that you think you can achieve using TCO analysis must be very strong because TCO analysis requires a big commitment of time and effort on your part, as well as on the part of many others in your organization. At every step of the way in a TCO project, you want to think about cost/benefit. Is it likely that the benefits of the analysis will outweigh the costs? If you answer no, TCO analysis is not recommended. If you can answer yes, then you need to identify whether the project you have chosen has the characteristics that are important in a successful TCO project.

Some of the characteristics that make a purchase, outsourcing analysis or process analysis well suited for TCO analysis include that the purchase is a relatively large spend amount, procurement believes the item has significant transaction costs associated with it that are not currently recognized, and there is an opportunity to have an impact on that spend area via negotiation, changing suppliers, or improving internal operations.

Capital purchases are virtually always good candidates for TCO analysis because after what appears to be a relatively large initial outlay, there continue to be costs associated with usage year after year and day after day. Leading organizations such as Johnson & Johnson do TCO analysis on major purchases, such as acquiring a fleet of vehicles. Intel uses TCO analysis on all of its capital equipment, especially the capital used in production. Other companies, such as Phillips, Heineken and Texas Instruments, have used it to select suppliers of parts and components when there are important differences in things such as quality, service, lead times and inventory levels. Imagine that a tech company like Sony is trying to determine where it should source a certain part for its Pencoed, Wales professional camera systems. Its goal would include more informed decision making, identification of cost reduction opportunities and perhaps more.

Step 2: Form a team to work on TCO analysis

Team formation will vary depending on the project under consideration. Sometimes, a team is formed during step 1 when a project is identified. The specific team membership may change as the TCO project is formed during step 1. At a minimum, the team should include procurement, users and any functional/technical experts. Finance/accounting should be part of the team to add credibility to the calculations. TCO analysis is best done in a team setting. Because TCO analysis is time-consuming and complex, it is important to gain the commitment and cooperation of others in advance. Before proceeding, it is also important to consider:

- What is in it for others?
- Why should they cooperate?
- How will it improve their job environment and company performance?
- Do we need top management sponsorship? Who and why?

Gaining participation of others in TCO analysis may require persuasion. In some cases, the organization might want to include supply chain members, such as key customers, suppliers or logistics providers if they have a significant impact on the TCO, or the outcome of the analysis may have a significant impact on them. In a supplier selection team like the one Sony would need in the example above, members might include engineering or design (since it is a high-tech item), procurement, manufacturing, logistics and others who might be affected or have important information about the process or potential suppliers.

Step 3: Identify relevant costs and gather data

At this step, the real work begins. It is important at this stage to keep the scope of the TCO analysis reasonable – to make sure benefits exceed cost. To really understand the costs associated with the supplier options, it is necessary to draw a process map or flow diagram for each option. This would include locations, time, costs and inventory levels at each step of the process.

The team uses the process flowcharts to help them with their brainstorming of cost drivers. Brainstorming is an excellent approach for coming up with a laundry list of possible cost elements that will later be narrowed down based on importance and impact. This list would include:

- price for items;
- quality levels;
- lead times;
- inventory levels;
- transportation, duties and tariffs;
- payment terms (impact cash flow and money tied up);
- damage in transit.

Note that the non-cost items will not be a part of the cost analysis. These issues will be discussed as 'soft costs' or other issues. Lead times are only a cost to the extent that the company must carry more inventory or have more obsolete items because of long lead times. In TCO, only costs that are incremental, and have a direct impact on the bottom line are included in the calculation. They are now ready to gather cost data.

Gathering the cost data can require a significant number of queries and even manual effort. When Intel is looking at manufacturing equipment, it must consider how that equipment interfaces with the other equipment used in production, defect rates produced by equipment, uptime, the frequency of required maintenance, capacity available versus capacity needed, and more. Most of the data needed is not readily available in the form needed in the accounting system. Most TCO analyses are conducted on spreadsheets because spreadsheets allow the flexibility to change as assumptions change, and have sufficient power to handle all but the most sophisticated TCO analysis. To make the comparison of alternatives meaningful, the costs will be translated to a cost per usable part. Costs must be gathered for each viable alternative.

Step 4: Fine-tune the TCO analysis, including sensitivity analysis

Many of the costs within the TCO model may be estimates. The team may have a 'range' of reasonable cost estimates for certain cost elements, such as transportation cost and damage. In that case, the team should do a 'sensitivity analysis', reanalysing the total model with different cost estimates to see how sensitive the model is to changes in those costs. What if volume increases or decreases significantly? How would that affect the price paid in each alternative? For capital equipment, how is the TCO per unit of output affected as volume changes? If our estimates are off by a small percentage, might another piece of equipment be preferred?

If the decision recommendation changes as the estimates change, the team should investigate those particular cost elements more carefully – trying to improve its level of confidence in its estimates. Again, this is a cost/benefit issue. How much time should we invest in getting very precise in certain cost elements that won't have any impact on the outcome of our analysis anyway? If the decision is unaffected as the estimate changes, it is probably not worth the time to refine the estimate for that variable. When the team is comfortable, it is ready to use the data in decision making, and/or present the results to top management. You need to be ready to answer all potential 'what if' questions from top management.

Step 5: Present recommendations to top management

Once the team is comfortable with the data, and has addressed areas of uncertainty through sensitivity analysis and additional data gathering, it is ready to prepare its presentation to management. This presentation should include the quantitative results of the TCO analysis, as well as other 'soft' factors that are more difficult to quantify. A good format to use for a report or presentation to top management includes:

- executive summary: includes brief background, summary of alternatives, key issues, TCO results, key sensitivities and recommendation;
- summary of TCO analysis results;
- sensitivities;
- non-cost issues;
- recommendations;
- appendices with detailed calculations and assumptions.

Once a TCO project is approved, it is important to monitor the implementation and actual results to learn about how to improve future processes. In addition, project documentation should be retained, preferably in a digital format, on an intranet or in the cloud, so that future TCO teams can benefit from the learnings of related projects.

Cost analysis

Cost analysis is a tool that complements both strategic cost management and total cost of ownership analysis. Cost analysis involves developing an understanding of the costs that underlie the items purchased – whether goods or services. This includes estimating the costs of labour, materials and components, cost of equipment, overhead and a reasonable profit margin. Understanding the cost structure helps the organization to understand whether it is paying a fair price. In addition, cost analysis sheds light on the cost drivers and potential areas for cost reduction, as well as whether it is appropriate to expect discounts for economies of scale achieved from volume increases. While entire books have been written about cost analysis, this section will focus on the basic principles rather than specific techniques.

We always conduct cost analysis with the customer in mind. What does the customer want and need, and how much are they willing to pay for it? What is the relative value of a feature versus its cost? To focus on cost alone would violate the principles of strategic cost management.

Level of detail and accuracy of cost analysis

There are three basic approaches to gathering data for cost analysis: roundtable, comparison and detailed analysis. In a roundtable approach, experts are brought together to develop the cost estimates, usually without detailed drawings or a bill of materials, and with limited information on specifications. Comparison estimating is based on determining the historical cost of the same or similar item as the one being estimated and adjusting or projecting the historical cost for future production. This comparison may be done at the cost element level or total price level. Detailed analysis estimating is characterized by a thorough review of all components, processes and assemblies. It is the most accurate of the three methods for estimating the direct cost of production. It is also the most time-consuming and expensive. The level of detail can be varied to meet your needs. Each of these approaches has advantages and disadvantages, as shown in Table 6.1.

Types of cost analysis

The three types of cost analysis presented here include target costing, should-cost analysis and supplier cost disclosure.

Target cost analysis is an approach used for new products, or major changes in products, where the organization, often led by sales or marketing, determines what they can afford to pay for the product based on their estimation of what the customer will pay, less the required profit margin. The costs are then allocated to the various cost categories – and suppliers are asked to try to meet or beat targets, sometimes with little relationship to what an item realistically should cost.

TABLE 6.1   Approaches to estimating cost for cost analysis

	Roundtable	Comparison	Detailed
Relative accuracy	Low because limited data used	Moderate/ high depending on data, technique and estimator	Moderate/ high depending on data, technique and estimator Balanced scorecard
Relative estimator consistency	Low different experts give different judgements	Moderate/ high depending on data, technique and estimator	High based on uniform application of principles
Relative speed of development	Fast little detailed analysis	Moderately fast especially with repetitive use	Slow requires detailed design and analysis cost
Relative development cost	Low fast and little data development cost	Moderate depending on need for data collection and analysis	High detailed design and analysis cost
Relative data required	Low based on expert judgement	Moderate only requires historical data	High requires detailed design and analysis

Should-cost analysis should always be the basis for developing your supplier negotiation and improvement plans when utilizing cost analysis. All of the variations in Table 6.1 are types of should-cost analysis because we are actually estimating what an item should cost, based on what is required to produce the item. A proactive should-cost analysis can be compared to the supplier's current practices to identify inefficiencies and recommend improvements.

Supplier cost disclosure involves asking a supplier to share its cost breakdown with you in order that you can better understand the cost drivers. Ideally, a buyer would use this to look for areas of improvement. However, suppliers fear that buyers will use this to negotiate leaner margins, so they are often hesitant to disclose, or may disclose false information. If you require a supplier to share this information, and force the issue, it is likely to hurt the relationship and result in false data. Supplier cost disclosure is most effective when the buyer and supplier have a close, long-term relationship built on trust. In addition, comparing supplier cost disclosure to should-cost data and/ or target cost data is a good way to check your own knowledge of the supplier's processes, and gain a deeper understanding in areas where your estimates are far from the supplier's actual costs.

Kaizen costing

Kaizen costing is a continuous improvement approach for cost management and reduction via waste reduction. Considered to be a basic element of all lean production and lean methods, kaizen aims for fast results. It is very compatible with the ideas of strategic cost management. Kaizen embraces the notion of including representatives at all levels, knowledge and skill sets within the company to contribute to improvements in cost and processes. It also presumes that nothing is ever perfect – systems and processes can always be improved upon. Value stream mapping and root-cause analysis, employing the five whys and other techniques help identify waste. For example, the five whys, largely credited to Toyota, asks the question 'why' five times in an effort to uncover underlying problems rather than simply treat their symptoms. When there is a problem, the five whys approach asks 'why'. For example:

'Why is the grass brown and dried out?'
'There is no rain and we have not been watering the grass.'

'Why haven't we been watering the grass?'
'Because the sprinkler system is leaking.'

'Why is it leaking?'
'Because the maintenance crew ran over one of the sprinkler heads while they were mowing.'

'Why?'
'Because that sprinkler head was sticking up above ground level.'

'Why?'
'Because the ground settled, and that sprinkler head became improperly elevated.'

CASE STUDY
Toyota manufacturing system

Kaizen costing is considered to be the heart of the Toyota Production System (TPS) (Toyota, nd). The TPS is a widely imitated and studied set of principles with the desired outcomes of providing:

- the customer with the highest quality vehicles, at the lowest possible cost, in a timely manner with the shortest possible lead times;

- team members with work satisfaction, job security and fair treatment;

- the company flexibility to respond to the market, achieve profit through cost reduction activities and long-term prosperity (Toyota, nd).

At Toyota Material Handling's European production sites, about 3,000 suggestions for improvements are received annually (Toyota, nd). This large number of suggestions is based on kaizen principles – those closest to the work are most familiar with the inefficiencies and problems in the processes. The Toyota Production System also embraces the notion of quality, cost and delivery. Thus, all kaizen – continuous improvement efforts – are aimed at constantly improving on quality, cost and delivery. Toyota emphasizes that all of its systems are customer-driven –based on the value proposition (Toyota, nd), just like strategic cost management.

Thus, we identify a solution to the problem – dig the sprinkler head placement deeper, and replace it.

Kaizen principles are applicable across profit and non-profit businesses, government, manufacturing and services. Toyota founded the Toyota Production System Support Center to 'contribute to society' by sharing the Toyota Production System and help improve North American Industries. Kaizen activities were applied to help several children's hospitals identify and solve a serious problem known as central line-associated bloodstream infections (CLABSIs). This occurs when a plastic tube is placed in a vein that goes directly to the heart. All the equipment was sterilized as in any medical procedure, yet this routine action kept leading to infections. After observing the process repeatedly, the Toyota volunteers found a pattern where some extra activities were occurring that were not included in the process, which were causing the problems. It developed a new, standardized process that included all the steps, and infections have been reduced by 75 per cent (Henshall, 2017). The United States Environmental Protection Agency recommends kaizen as an important tool to contribute to waste reduction and enhance environmental performance (USEPA, nd).

Summary and conclusions

Strategic cost management is an important process for improving an organization's outcomes – both in terms of meeting customer needs and reducing costs. It is a holistic process that embraces new product development as well as ongoing improvements. To ensure that the costs data used in decision making are accurate and meaningful, strategic cost management should be based on total cost of ownership analysis and understanding underlying costs through cost analysis. Strategic cost management is completely compatible with kaizen costing. It represents an important way for procurement to contribute strategically to the organization.

References

Amazon (2020) 2019 Annual Report, 31 January, https://s2.q4cdn.com/299287126/files/doc_financials/2020/ar/2019-Annual-Report.pdf (archived at https://perma.cc/W6VY-9VKT)

Amazon (2021) Who we are, https://www.aboutamazon.com/about-us (archived at https://perma.cc/R5NQ-NU5N)

Berman, J (2021) Amazon announces purchase of 11 new aircraft, in move to expand transportation fleet, *Supply Chain Management Review*, 6 January, https://www.scmr.com/article/amazon_announces_purchase_of_11_new_aircraft_in_move_to_expand_transportati (archived at https://perma.cc/T48A-R4RA)

Coombs, C (2017) Amazon to spend $200M for one of its most expensive fulfilment centers ever, *Puget Sound Business Journal*, 9 June, https://www.bizjournals.com/seattle/news/2017/06/09/amazon-to-spend-200m-on-fulfillment-center-for-130.html (archived at https://perma.cc/7XQ9-93ZZ)

Cooper, R and Slagmulder, R (1998) Strategic cost management: what is strategic cost management? *Management Accounting*, 76 (1), pp 14–16

Hartmans, A (2021) 'Amazon' wasn't the original name of Jeff Bezos' company, and 14 other little-known facts about the early days of Amazon, *Insider*, 3 February, http://www.businessinsider.com/jeff-bezos-amazon-history-facts-2017-4 (archived at https://perma.cc/97NX-FGHV)

Henshall, A (2017) How Toyota saved children's lives with process implementation, Business 2 Community, 13 October, https://www.business2community.com/trends-news/toyota-saved-childrens-lives-process-implementation-01931628 (archived at https://perma.cc/9SBK-6PD8)

IBM (2013) IBM Archives: Chronological history of IBM, http://www-03.ibm.com/ibm/history/history/decade_1910.html (archived at https://perma.cc/78EM-C7CG)

Kucera, D (2013) Why Amazon is on a warehouse building spree, *Bloomberg BusinessWeek*, 29 August, http://www.businessweek.com/articles/2013-08-29/why-amazon-is-on-a-warehouse-building-spree (archived at https://perma.cc/8FY4-4KS4) [accessed 13 January 2021]

McCorvey, J J (2013) AmazonFresh is Jeff Bezos' last mile quest for total retail domination, Fast Company, 5 August, http://www.fastcompany.com/3014817/amazon-jeff-bezos (archived at https://perma.cc/4BLJ-Z6DJ)

Mission Statement.com (2021) IBM mission and vision statement analysis, https://mission-statement.com/ibm/ (archived at https://perma.cc/Z6JL-S3VT)

Office Timeline (2020) Amazon history timeline, 17 June, https://www.officetimeline.com/blog/amazon-history-timeline (archived at https://perma.cc/3H85-BH7B)

Porter, M (1985) *Competitive Advantage: Creating and sustaining superior performance*, Free Press, New York

Toyota (nd) Valuing the Toyota Production System and lean manufacturing, https://
www.toyotaforklift.com/resource-library/material-handling-solutions/products/
valuing-the-toyota-production-system-and-lean-manufacturing (archived at
https://perma.cc/9WLJ-P2VS)

USEPA (nd) Lean thinking and methods – kaizen, United States Environmental
Protection Agency, https://www.epa.gov/lean/lean-thinking-and-methods-kaizen
(archived at https://perma.cc/F33S-4JCS)

07

The impact of procurement on financial results

DR SIMON TEMPLAR

This chapter explores the relationship between procurement and financial performance (FP) by answering this question: How can procurement enhance value for its organization?

Procurement decisions relate to both capital (non-current assets) and revenue expenditure (operating expenditure). These decisions impact on your organization's income statement, balance sheet and associated financial ratios, and also on your customers' and suppliers' FP. Typical frameworks used to measure FP are introduced, including return on total assets minus current liabilities (ROTA – CL), shareholder value (SV) and earnings before interest and tax after asset charge (EAC), and their relationship to decisions taken by procurement are evaluated. Supply chain finance is introduced, an area of increasing importance to procurement practitioners. Finally, we present three data analytical approaches that can bridge the gap between the physical, information and financial flows in the supply chain (SC), and increasing functional integration within an organization's intra- and inter-SC operation.

Procurement and value creation

Procurement has a direct impact on a firm's competitive advantage, and you need to recognize this significant relationship, as it provides you with a direct link to the board that communicates the impact of your decisions on financial performance and value creation (VC). Interestingly, Porter (1985) identifies procurement as a support function, however Ellram and Liu (2002: 30) argue that purchasing and supply chain management (SCM) decisions are not just concerned with reducing cost, but are fundamental to the organization's financial performance: 'The financial impact of purchasing and supply management goes well beyond cost reduction. It extends to such critical performance areas as business growth, profitability, cash flow, and asset utilization.'

Ellram and Liu (2002: 30) maintain that if procurement wishes to be seen as a strategic function within the organization, they need to be able to highlight their value-adding potential, by arguing their strategic role in a language that the board will understand and relate to, a financial justification: 'Supply chain managers need to be able to quantify that broader impact. And then convey that message upward so that top management better understands how purchasing and supply management can contribute to company success.'

Ryals and McDonald (2008: 266) concur with Ellram and Liu (2002) that the role of procurement is an enabler of value creation, but add that inferior procurement decisions can also destroy value: 'There are many examples of transactions where the cheapest product or service turns out to be of poorer value than buying a more expensive product which lasts longer and requires less maintenance.'

We have all taken purchasing decisions, for instance buying a motor car or inkjet printer, based on the initial purchase price, to find that over time the additional costs associated with the purchasing decision have cost us more,[1] and only to be told annoyingly that 'you only get what you paid for'. Hindsight is a valuable commodity, but in short supply. Therefore, procurement has to take a holistic view when making purchasing decisions, and certainly if these decisions are long term, for instance sourcing non-current assets (NCA) or

TABLE 7.1   Procurement initiatives

Category	Procurement initiative
People	Investing and developing procurement expertise and capabilities, and sponsoring professional and academic qualifications in procurement.
Portfolio	Collaborating with suppliers to design and develop new products.
Partners	Introducing supplier relationship management and supplier programmes that share information across organizational boundaries.
Planet	Adopting corporate social responsibility initiatives underpinned by total cost of ownership. Introducing supplier audits.
Profit	Introducing procurement programmes and projects that have a positive impact on the drivers of shareholder value such as vendor-managed inventory and target costing, therefore reducing the cost to supply.
Productivity	Introduce procurement key performance indicators (KPIs) that are goal congruent with the organization's strategic objectives.

entering into long-term third-party contracts with suppliers. Table 7.1 shows a selection of procurement initiatives, which illustrate the diverse role that procurement has within an organization. I would also argue that procurement decisions cross functional boundaries, for example recruitment decisions.

Procurement decisions and types of expenditure

There are two types of sourcing decisions made by procurement. The first is capital expenditure on long-term non-current assets (NCA), such as property, plant and equipment (PPE). Expenditure on NCA can be differentiated further into two types: tangible and intangible. Tangible assets are physical objects such as trucks and sheds, and other supply chain infrastructure. However, intangible assets are non-physical in nature, for example goodwill: it has a monetary value, it can be found on the balance sheet but you cannot see or touch it – other examples include trademarks and licences.

The second decision is to procure goods and services that will be consumed in the current accounting period (short-term) such as fuel

TABLE 7.2   Capital and revenue expenditure

Capital	Revenue
Trucks	Wages
Trailers	Utilities
Material handling equipment	Material handling equipment rental
Distribution centre	Third-party logistics fees
Information technology	Packaging materials
Fixtures and fittings	Agency workers

for trucks and raw materials/components used in the production process, referred to as revenue expenditure. Typical examples of capital and revenue expenditure related to supply chain management are illustrated in Table 7.2. The list is not exhaustive – I expect that you can think of many more examples.

Procurement decisions and accounting policy

Reading this section is not going to turn you into an accountant, but it is important that you are aware of how revenue and capital procurement decisions are treated by accountants, and how they impact on the income statement and balance sheet and the financial performance measures that ultimately measure your role in creating value for your business.[2] We are going to focus on two areas of accounting policy, important when evaluating the financial performance of potential suppliers. The method of inventory valuation (IV) and depreciation policy adopted by your supplier will have a significant financial impact on:

- gross profit (GP);
- earnings before interest and tax (EBIT).

Gross profit calculation

The gross profit (GP) for any business is calculated by subtracting the cost of goods sold (COGS) for the financial period from the sales revenue (SR) for the same accounting period. The COGS is calculated by adding the opening inventory at the start of the accounting period to the purchases that have been made during the financial year, finally subtracting the value of the closing inventory to give the COGS (Table 7.3).

In the example (Table 7.3), the GP is $100 million with a gross margin (GM) of 50 per cent. Gross margin is calculated by dividing gross profit by sales revenue and multiplying by 100. Procurement has a major impact on this ratio, as they are responsible for purchases and supply chain managers are responsible for inventory management (IM). A significant factor that will have a major impact on the GP calculation is the inventory valuation (IV) method used.

Inventory valuation methods

The most commonly used methods for inventory valuation are first in first out (FIFO), last in first out (LIFO) and average cost (AVCO). We will now explore them in more depth using a fictitious example to calculate an organization's closing inventory valuation and demonstrate the impact of each method on the company's gross margin. The strict rule regarding the valuation of inventory in the financial statements is

TABLE 7.3   Gross profit calculation

Trading account for year ending 31 March XX	$m	$m
Sales revenue		200
Less cost of goods sold		
Opening inventory	45	
Plus purchases	85	
	130	
Less closing inventory	30	100
Gross profit		100

as follows: inventory should be valued at cost; however if the net realizable value (NRV) is less than cost (because of mark-downs, damages or obsolescence), then the NRV is used. The difference between the original cost and NRV is written off in the income statement.

FIRST IN FIRST OUT (FIFO)

The FIFO methodology uses a traditional inventory rotation policy where the first goods received are the first to be issued, therefore deriving the closing IV. Table 7.4 illustrates the opening inventory value, the receipts, the issues and the closing IV for the accounting period. Under FIFO the closing IV is $12,500 or $25 per unit.

LAST IN FIRST OUT (LIFO)

The LIFO method is the opposite of FIFO. The goods received last into the distribution centre are the first to be issued and the IV is calculated in Table 7.5.

AVERAGE COST (AVCO)

The final IV method is AVCO, which adopts the principles of FIFO with regard to IM but applies a weighted average to work out the IV. Every time goods are issued and received the inventory valuation is

TABLE 7.4   Inventory valuation: FIFO

Receipts			Issues			Balance		
Units	Price	Total	Units	Price	Total	Units	Price	Total
						500	15.00	7,500
			400	50	20,000	100	15.00	1,500
600	20	12,000				600	20.00	12,000
						700		13,500
			400	50	20,000	300	20.00	6,000
600	25	15,000				600	25.00	15,000
						900		21,000
			400	50	20,000	500	25.00	12,500

TABLE 7.5   Inventory valuation: LIFO

Receipts			Issues			Balance		
Units	Price	Total	Units	Price	Total	Units	Price	Total
						500	15.00	7,500
			400	50	20,000	100	15.00	1,500
600	20	12,000				600	20.00	12,000
						700		13,500
			400	50	20,000	200	20.00	4,000
						100	15.00	1,500
						300		5,500
600	25	15,000				600	25.00	15,000
						200	20.00	4,000
						100	15.00	1,500
						900		20,500
			400	50	20,000	200	25.00	5,000
						200	20.00	4,000
						100	15.00	1,500
						500		10,500

TABLE 7.6   Inventory valuation AVCO

Receipts			Issues			Balance		
Units	Price	Total	Units	Price	Total	Units	Price	Total
						500	15.00	7,500
			400	50	20,000	100	15.00	1,500
600	20	12,000				600	20.00	12,000
						700	19.29	13,500
			400	50	20,000	300	19.29	5,786
600	25	15,000				600	25.00	15,000
						900	23.10	20,786
			400	50	20,000	500	23.10	11,548

recalculated as illustrated in Table 7.6. The closing IV under this method is $11,548 and $23.10 per unit.

In Table 7.7 each IV approach is compared, showing that they each produce a different closing IV. This impacts not only on the organization's cost of goods sold, but also its gross profit. The LIFO produces the lowest closing inventory value, the highest costs of goods sold figure and the lowest gross profit, resulting in the lowest gross margin of 60 per cent. However, with FIFO it is the opposite, resulting in the highest gross margin of 63.33 per cent, and AVCO falls between both methods with a gross margin of 61.75 per cent. Whichever approach an organization adopts, procurement decisions related to the price paid for the inventory will have an impact on the cost of goods sold and the gross margin calculation.

Earnings before interest and tax (EBIT)

The purpose of depreciation (tangible) and amortization (intangible) is to match the expenditure on non-current assets (NCA) over their useful life and therefore against the sales revenue (SR) by these assets. It is essential that you are aware that depreciation has no effect on cash flow, as the cash left the business to purchase the NCA in the

TABLE 7.7 Inventory valuation comparison

	FIFO		LIFO		AVCO	
	$	$	$	$	$	$
Sales		60,000		60,000		60,000
Less cost of goods sold						
Opening inventory	7,500		7,500		7,500	
add purchases	27,000		27,000		27,000	
less closing inventory	12,500	22,000	10,500	24,000	11,548	22,952
Gross profit		38,000		36,000		37,048

first place; it is an accounting adjustment to derive profit for an accounting period.

The choice of depreciation method will have an impact on an organization's operating expenses and hence its EBIT. For instance, the straight-line method (SLM) will charge an equal amount of depreciation each year to the income statement, while the reducing balance method (RBM) charges a higher proportion of depreciation in the earlier years of the NCA's life. The case study illustrates this point.

CASE STUDY

Alpha PLC

Alpha PLC has purchased a non-current asset worth $5 million. It will have a useful life of five years and on disposal its value will be $1 million, so the total depreciation will be $4 million. Figure 7.1 illustrates the annual depreciation charge in the income statement for both methods.

FIGURE 7.1   Annual depreciation charge by method

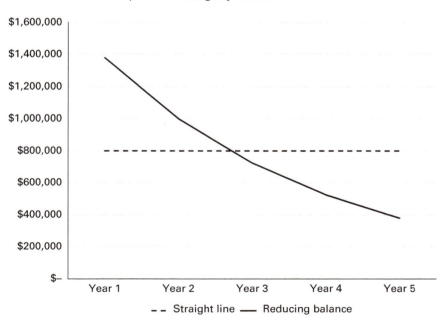

FIGURE 7.2 Depreciation method and EBIT percentage

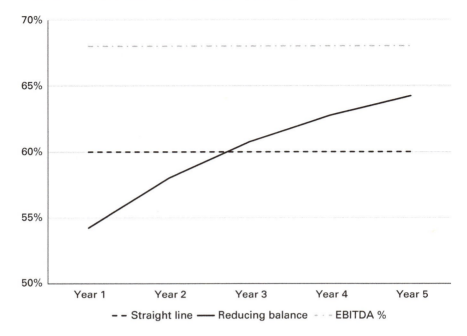

Let's assume that Alpha's revenue is $10 million, their operating expenses are $3.2 million (excluding depreciation) and they remain constant over five years. In Figure 7.2 we can see the impact that each depreciation method has on Alpha's EBIT percentage.

The RBM has a lower EBIT percentage in the early years but produces a higher percentage later on, whereas the SLM produces a constant EBIT percentage over the period. Earnings before tax, interest, depreciation and amortization (EBITDA) percentage ignores depreciation and therefore cancels out the impact of different depreciation methods.[3]

When buyers are comparing the profitability of their suppliers, they should compare traditional profit measures such as gross margin and EBIT, but also apply EBITDA.

Ratio analysis: understanding the financial health of your supplier

There is an old saying: 'Look before you leap'. In other words, do your research before entering into a relationship with a potential supplier. There are numerous financial questions that procurement practitioners need to ask when evaluating a potential new supplier, relating to profitability, liquidity and efficiency.

Financial ratios can provide you with valuable information about your prospective supplier, but they are not foolproof; they make use of historical information, and remember the old adage from investment analysts, 'past performance is not a guarantee of future performance'. Therefore you should triangulate your research with other data sources such as supplier references, case studies and interviews with other customers that have been supplied by the vendor. These are valuable sources of evidence of supplier performance. Alternatively, you can outsource your supplier evaluation to organizations that specialize in this area.

Financial ratios can be derived from source data in the income statement, the balance sheet or a combination of the two, as illustrated in Figure 7.3. However, it is important that procurement practitioners understand where the source data is derived from, what the ratios are measuring and, more important, how the decisions that they take impact on the ratios and the overall financial performance of their organization.

FIGURE 7.3 Financial ratios and financial statements

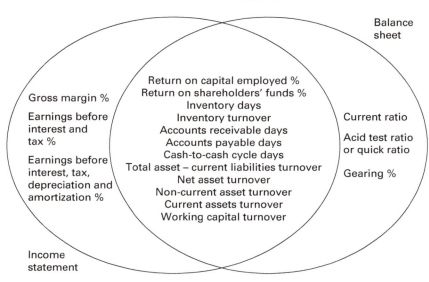

SOURCE Adapted from Templar (2019:198)

TABLE 7.8 Financial ratios

Category	Ratio
Profitability	Gross margin
	Earnings before interest and tax %
	Earnings before interest, tax, depreciation and amortization %
	Return on capital employed %
	Return on shareholders' funds %
Liquidity	Current ratio
	Acid test ratio or quick ratio
Working capital	Inventory days
	Inventory turnover
	Accounts receivable days or Days sales outstanding
	Accounts payable days or Days payable outstanding
	Cash to cash cycle days
Efficiency	Total asset turnover
	Net asset turnover
	Total net asset turnover
	Non-current asset turnover
	Current assets turnover
	Working capital turnover
Financial structure	Gearing %

In this section, we focus on a set of financial ratios that can be used to analyse organizational and financial performance. Table 7.8 illustrates a set of typical financial ratios and their financial performance categories. This list is not exhaustive but provides you with an introduction to the different types of financial ratios.

For each ratio, its method of calculation will be illustrated. The ratios will be calculated using data extracted from the financial statements of Beta PLC.

BETA PLC

Income statement	$m	Balance sheet	$m
Sales revenue	200	Non-current assets	
Less cost of goods sold	100	Property, plant and equipment	220
Gross profit	100		220
Operating expenses	42	Current assets	

Operating profit	58	Inventory	30
Finance costs	8	Accounts receivables	40
Earnings before tax	50	Cash	10
Corporation tax	20		80
Earnings after tax	30	Total assets	300
Dividend	10		
Retained profit for the year	20	Equity	
		$1 Ordinary shares	50
		Retained earnings	100
			150
		Non-current liabilities	
		Long-term loan	100
			100
		Current liabilities	
		Accounts payable	25
		Dividends payable	5
		Taxation	10
		Overdraft	10
			50
		Total liabilities	150
		Total equity and liabilities	300

PROFITABILITY RATIOS

Table 7.9 illustrates profitability ratios using data extracted from Beta PLC's financial statements. The gross margin percentage, EBITDA percentage and EBIT percentage, which only use the income statement, measure how sales revenue (top line) has been eroded by costs as we travel down the income statement. For instance, you have heard the question 'what's the impact on the bottom line?' This is the retained profit for the year, which in Beta's case is $20 million (10 per cent); 90 per cent of sales revenue has been eroded by some form of cost. You can now see how your procurement decisions can make a

TABLE 7.9 Beta PLC profitability ratios

Ratio	Formula	Calculation
Gross margin (GM %)	*(Gross profit/sales revenue) * 100*	($100m/$200m) * 100 = 50%
Earnings before interest and tax, depreciation and amortization percentage(EBITDA %)	*(Earnings before interest, tax, depreciation and amortization/ sales revenue) * 100*	($64m/$200m) * 100 = 32%F023
Earnings before interest and tax percentage (EBIT %)	*(Earnings before interest and tax/ sales revenue) * 100*	($58m/$200m) * 100 = 29%
Return on capital employed percentage(ROCE %)	*(Earnings before interest and tax/ capital employed) * 100*	($58m/$250m) * 100 = 23.2%
Return on shareholder funds percentage (ROSF %)	*(Earnings after tax/shareholders' funds) * 100*	($30m/$150m) * 100 = 20%

NOTE #Beta PLC's annual depreciation is $6m, which is included in their operating expenses.

difference to the bottom line. The other two ratios measure the return generated by different classifications of capital and we will examine later on in this chapter.

LIQUIDITY RATIOS

Table 7.10 illustrates two liquidity ratios for Beta PLC. The current ratio compares the value of current assets to current liabilities. Beta's ratio is 1.6 to 1.0, which means that for every $1 of current liabilities Beta has $1.60 of current assets to cover their short-term liabilities. With the acid test or quick ratio, inventory is not included as the assumption is that inventories take time to be turned into cash, hence Beta's AT ratio is 1.0 to 1.0. Traditionally accounting texts have suggested benchmarks of 2.0 to 1.0 for the current ratio and 1.0 to 1.0 for the acid test ratio for manufacturing companies; however, it does depend on industrial sector and cash flow.

An issue to flag up, especially for procurement practitioners, is the 'liquidity paradox'. If your organization is focusing on reducing inventory levels on its balance sheet, it can weaken its current ratio.

TABLE 7.10 Beta PLC liquidity ratios

Ratio	Formula	Calculation
Current ratio	*Current assets: Current liabilities*	$80m : $50m = 1.6 : 1.0
Acid test ratio	*(Current assets – Inventory): Current liabilities*	($80m – $30m) : $50m= 1.0 : 1.0

WORKING CAPITAL RATIOS

Table 7.11 illustrates five important working capital ratios that you need to know when evaluating a potential supplier.

Inventory days, which measures the average number of days inventory is held by the organization, is derived from the company's cost of goods sold calculation. Beta's inventory days are 137. Procurement decisions influencing inventory management, purchasing and the economic order quantity will have a positive impact on this ratio, but you must consider the impact of inventory decisions on other functions such as sales and marketing with regard to customer service, lead times and product variety.

Inventory turnover (IT) measures the velocity of inventory within the business. It is calculated by dividing 365 days by the inventory days to produce a multiplier. The IT for Beta PLC is 2.66, which means the company on average turns over its inventory 2.66 times a year.

TABLE 7.11 Working capital ratios

Ratio	Formula	Calculation
Inventory days	*(Average inventory/Cost of sales) * 365*	($37.5m/$100m) * 365 = 137 days
Inventory turnover	*365/Inventory days*	365/137 = 2.66
Accounts receivable days	*(Average receivables/Credit sales) * 365*	($40m/$200m) * 365 = 73 days
Accounts payable days	*(Average payables/Credit purchases) * 365*	($25m/$85m) * 365 = 107 days
Cash to cash cycle days	*Inventory days + Accounts receivable days – Accounts payable days*	137 + 73 – 107 = 103 days

Accounts receivable days (or days sales outstanding) monitors the average time in days taken for the business's credit customers to pay them. It is derived from the credit sales from the income statement and the accounts receivable on the balance sheet. Decisions related to credit control and terms and conditions can have a favourable impact on this ratio, as can the use of supply chain finance initiatives. Currently Beta's customers, on average, pay them in 73 days.

Accounts payable days (or days payable outstanding) measure the time it takes the company to pay its suppliers. It is calculated by taking the average accounts payable and dividing it by the credit purchases. By extending its accounts payable time, an organization can derive a cash flow benefit; however, this can have an impact on its suppliers' liquidity and lead to financial distress, endangering the financial sustainability of the chain. Supply chain finance instruments are increasingly being deployed in this space and is an area of increasing interest for the procurement function as they manage the relationship with suppliers. In the case of Beta PLC, they pay their suppliers, on average, in around 107 days. Suppliers will be monitoring the buyers' accounts payable days when evaluating whether to do business with them, and recently companies that have extended the time taken, or simply take a long time, to pay suppliers have been named and shamed in the media, which has reputational implications.

The cash-to-cash cycle time measures the time taken for the business to recoup its cash back. Beta has to wait 103 days to recoup its cash back, hence it has a liquidity gap, which will need to be reduced by:

- liberating cash tied up in inventories;
- cutting the time taken by their customers to pay them;
- extending the payment terms to their suppliers.

EFFICIENCY RATIOS

The efficiency ratios in Table 7.12 illustrate the proportion of sales revenue generated from different classifications of the organization's assets. The formula for each ratio is based on a standard approach, where sales revenue is divided by the asset classification to generate a multiplier. For instance, the total assets turnover is calculated by dividing sales revenue ($200 million) by the value of total assets

TABLE 7.12 Beta PLC efficiency ratios

Ratio	Formula	Calculation
Total assets (TA) turnover	*Sales revenue/Total assets*	$200m/$300m = 0.67
Total assets – Current liabilities turnover	*Sales revenue/Total assets – Current liabilities*	$200m/$250m = 0.80
Total net asset turnover	*Sales revenue/Total net assets*	$200m/$150m = 1.33
Non-current asset (NCA) turnover	*Sales revenue/Non-current assets*	$200m/$220m = 0.91
Current asset (CA) turnover	*Sales revenue/Current assets*	$200m/$80m = 2.50
Working capital (WC) turnover	*Sales revenue/Working capital*	$200m/$30m = 6.67

($300 million), to give a ratio of 0.67, which means that every $1 of total assets generates 67 cents in sales revenue. These ratios can be used to compare the financial performance of different asset classifications in terms of sales revenue generation for different organizations in an industrial sector.

Procurement decisions that are able to reduce an organization's total assets will improve efficiency ratios. These include:

• outsourcing non-current assets;

• leasing or renting non-current assets;

• vendor-managed inventory;

• postponement.

FINANCIAL STRUCTURE RATIO

The gearing ratio measures the value of non-current liabilities as a percentage of capital employed. In the case of Beta PLC, 40 per cent of capital employed is funded by non-current liabilities (long-term debt) of $100 million.

WEAKNESS OF FINANCIAL RATIOS

When comparing an organization's financial ratios, it is fundamentally important that you are comparing like with like; if not, your analysis will be flawed. There are many factors that need to be taken into consideration when comparing financial performance using financial ratios. They include:

- accounting policies adopted by the organizations;
- previous trends cannot be relied on for future financial performance;
- economic conditions (growth, risk and inflation) may vary with regard to the geographical location.

Measuring financial performance

It is extremely important that you understand the financial implications of your decisions on the financial statements of your organization, and that you are able to discuss and demonstrate their impact with the finance function. This section will introduce to you three frameworks typically used in practice for measuring financial performance; they are return on total assets minus current liabilities (ROTA – CL), shareholder value (SV) and EBIT after asset charge (EAC).

Return on total assets minus current liabilities (ROTA – CL)

ROTA – CL has traditionally been used as a barometer of financial performance. It is calculated by taking the EBIT and dividing it by the value of the organization's total assets minus current liabilities (TA – CL)on their balance sheet and multiplying by 100 to give a percentage.[4] ROTA – CL uses the top half of the balance sheet (where the money has gone to), while return on capital employed (ROCE) focuses on the bottom half (where the money has come from) – have a look at Beta's balance sheet. Procurement practitioners make decisions related to the top half of the balance sheet with regard to non-current assets, current assets and current liabilities. However, Brookson (2001:43) highlights the importance of the ROTA – CL/ROCE ratio:

> ...reveals how much profit is being made on the money invested in the business and is a key measure of how well management is doing its job.

Beta PLC's EBIT is $58 million; divided by $250 million, this produces a ROTA – CL of 23.2 per cent. However, the ratio can also be derived by multiplying two other ratios together; these are the total assets minus current liabilities turnover ratio (0.8) and EBIT interest percentage (29 per cent) as illustrated in Figure 7.4. This relationship between these financial ratios is extremely important for procurement practitioners, as they are able to influence both ratios by the decisions they take as they influence sales, cost of goods sold, operating expenses (OPEX), non-current assets, current assets and current liabilities.

Figure 7.4 depicts the relationship between Beta's income statement, balance sheet and ROTA – CL. If inventory could be reduced by 50 per cent by adopting vendor-managed inventory and the resulting cash savings are used to reduce non-current liabilities, what would be the impact on the ROTA – CL percentage? Inventory would be reduced to $15 million and therefore TA – CL is reduced to $235 million, if EBIT stays constant at $58 million. (You could also have savings related to the cost of holding inventory, which would improve the EBIT percentage, then ROTA – CL would be 24.7 per cent, an increase of 6.5 per cent.)

As an example, let's suppose Beta PLC outsources its logistics operation to a third-party logistics organization, taking $30 million of non-current assets off its balance sheet and is operating-cost neutral; this would increase ROTA – CL to 26.4 per cent, an increase of 13.8 per cent.

The key takeaway is that your procurement decision can impact on both the income statement and the balance sheet.

Shareholder value

The UK's Chartered Institute of Management Accountants terminology (CIMA, 2005: 96) defines shareholder return as:

> Total return to the shareholders in terms of both dividends and share price growth, calculated as the present value of future free cash flows of the business discounted at the weighted average cost of the capital of the business less the market value of its debt.

FIGURE 7.4 ROTA – CL

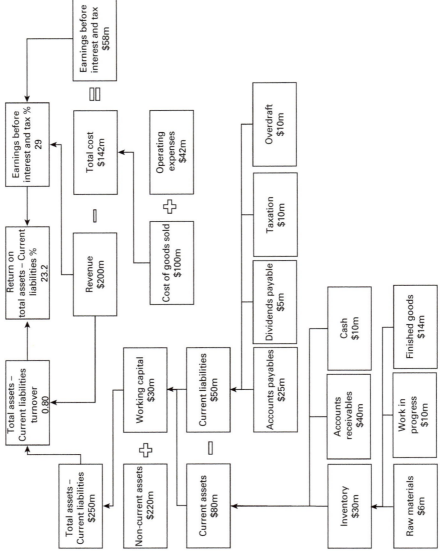

Lukas *et al* (2005: 414) highlight the significant role that managers have in enhancing shareholder value and its importance in maintaining an organization's financial sustainability:

> Increasingly, the rhetoric used by top managers and boards is that the primary task of management is to maximize returns to shareholders.

Selecting an inappropriate supplier, or procuring the wrong product or component can be a financial disaster for any organization, as it can seriously damage their reputation, impact on future sales revenue and be expensive to put right, in terms of fines, compensation and additional process costs, therefore eroding profitability, reducing cash flow and destroying shareholder value, making the business less attractive for future investors.

Christopher (2011: 63) identified five drivers of shareholder value. Table 7.13 presents these drivers and matches them to appropriate procurement and supply chain initiatives.

TABLE 7.13 Shareholder value drivers and procurement initiatives

Shareholder value driver	Procurement initiative
Revenue growth	• New product development • Target pricing • Supplier audits
Operating cost reduction	• Vendor-managed inventory • Make or buy • Supplier relationship management • Standardized components • Inventory holding costs • Returns management • Managing inventory write-offs
Tax minimization	• Tax-efficient supply chain management • Customs and excise duties
Fixed capital efficiency	• Outsourcing • Total cost of ownership • Leasing or alternative financing arrangements
Working capital efficiency	• Inventory management • Postponement • Cash to cash velocity • Supply chain finance

SOURCE Christopher (2011)

Therefore, the aim of procurement decisions should be to increase cash-to-cash velocity and cash retention, which will enhance shareholder value.

EBIT after asset charge (EAC)

EAC can be used as a proxy for economic profit. The organization will only add value if their EBIT exceeds the opportunity cost of the capital invested in the business. When this occurs then the organization has added value.

CASE STUDY
Deutsche Post DHL Group

One organization that has adopted EBIT as a performance metric is Deutsche Post World Net (2007: 8):

> We are introducing EBIT after asset charge as a new primary performance metric to focus all divisions on sustained value growth. From 1 January 2008, management incentives will also be tied to this metric. In this way, we aim to improve cash generation.

The motivation for adopting this approach was stated in the organization's 2013 annual report (Deutsche Post DHL Group, 2013: 50):

> Making the asset charge a part of business decisions encourages all divisions to use resources efficiently and ensures that the operating business is geared towards increasing value sustainably whilst generating cash flow.

TABLE 7.14 EAC calculation for the Deutsche Post DHL Group

Year	2015	2016	2017	2018	2019
EBIT €m	2,411	3,491	3,741	3,162	4,128
Asset charge €m	1,534	1,528	1,566	2,446	2,619
EAC €m	877	1,963	2,175	716	1,509
WACC	8.50%	8.50%	8.50%	8.50%	8.50%

SOURCE Deutsche Post DHL (2016, 2018, 2019)

Table 7.14 illustrates the EAC calculation for the Deutsche Post DHL Group over the five years between 2015 and 2019. The organization has generated earnings greater than their weighted average cost of capital (WACC) of 8.5 per cent.

Financially sustainable supply networks

Sourcing decisions will have an impact on the organization's working capital. Working capital is the difference between a business's current assets (short-term[5] assets such as inventory) and its current liabilities (short-term liabilities including accounts payable). Procurement decisions will impact on the level and value of inventory disclosed in the balance sheet. Furthermore, procurement has an impact on the accounts payable revealed in current liabilities on the balance sheet, as procurement will be involved in negotiating the terms and conditions between the organization and its suppliers, including the time period in which their suppliers are paid.

Extending payment days

Beta's cash-to-cash (C2C) cycle time is currently 103 days. If Beta reduce their inventory days and accounts receivable days by 5 per cent and extend their accounts payable by a similar percentage, we can see the impact on their C2C cycle is reduced by reduction of 16 days, which equates to a 15.5 per cent improvement (see Table 7.15).

An organization can improve its C2C cycle time by extending the time it takes to pay its suppliers. In effect it is using its accounts

TABLE 7.15 Beta PLC C2C cycle time initiative

Ratio	Original	5% Improvement
Inventory days	137	130
Accounts receivable days	73	69
Accounts payable days	107	112
Cash-to-cash cycle days	103	87

payable as short-term financing to improve its liquidity and cash flow. However, it is important to recognize that there is a potential downside to extending payment days, which will impact on the organization's reputation; we have all seen the headlines in financial press when companies are shamed for treating their suppliers poorly. This policy could have a profound risk on the financial sustainability of your organization's supply chain, increasing your risk should a key supplier suffer financial distress and go bankrupt. If a suitable supplier can't be found and you don't have sufficient inventory then there is a risk of significant disruption, not only to your operations but, more importantly, to your customer base as illustrated in Figure 7.5.

Supply chain finance

The Euro Banking Association (2014: 44) defines supply chain finance as:

> The use of financial instruments, practices and technologies to optimize the management of the working capital and liquidity tied up in supply chain processes for collaborating business partners.

FIGURE 7.5   Financially sustainable supply chain network

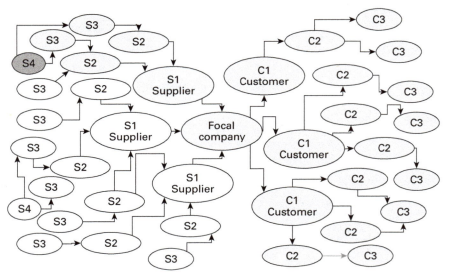

SOURCE Templar *et al* (2016: 68)

FIGURE 7.6 Overview of supply chain finance solutions

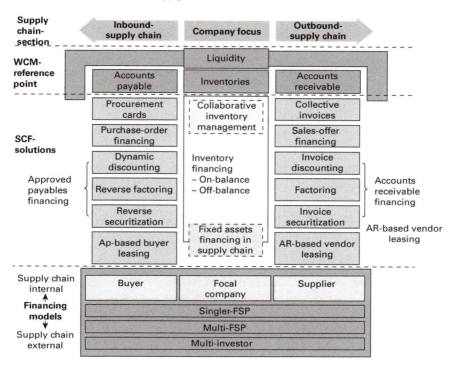

SOURCE Templar *et al* (2020)

In Figure 7.6, Templar *et al* (2020: 227) provide an overview of the variety of supply chain finance solutions differentiated by WC.[6]

Let's now focus on one supply chain finance instrument in more detail: dynamic discounting (DD), which is used by buyers to improve their C2C cycle time.

DYNAMIC DISCOUNTING (DD)

Dynamic discounting is a supply chain finance instrument that is used by the buyer to manage their accounts payable with their suppliers. The Euro Banking Association (2014: 48) defines dynamic discounting as follows:

> Dynamic discounting offers suppliers the early receipt of accounts payable due from a buyer in return for a variable discount. Typically, the funds are provided by the buyer from its own liquid resources.

The following fictitious example describes the DD approach (adapted from Templar, 2019).

CASE STUDY
Ultra Ltd

Ultra Ltd, a supplier to Mega Ltd, has been onboarded to Mega's DD programme. Mega Ltd's standard terms and conditions state that suppliers will be paid in 90 days, once the invoice has been approved for payment. However, if Ultra Ltd decides to take an early payment, they can, but their invoice value will be discounted; if they don't need the cash, the invoice will carry on to its due payment date. Table 7.16 illustrates the Mega Ltd DD calculation. If Ultra Ltd requires an invoice to be paid immediately then they will receive 95 per cent of its face value; however, if they require the invoice to be paid after 40 days they will receive 97.22 per cent of its value.

Ultra Ltd's treasury function can use the curve in Figure 7.7 to establish the percentage discount value of an invoice for a given early payment.

Currently Ultra Ltd has five invoices that have been approved for payment on Mega Ltd's supply chain finance platform. Table 7.17 illustrates for Ultra Ltd the current value of their discounting invoices on the system at this moment in time. If Ultra Ltd now decide to opt for earlier payment of all their invoices in the

TABLE 7.16   Mega Ltd DD rates

Payment days	Net invoice value %	Discount %
0	95.00	5.00
10	95.56	4.44
20	96.11	3.89
30	96.67	3.33
40	97.22	2.78
50	97.78	2.22
60	98.33	1.67
70	98.89	1.11
80	99.44	0.56
90	100.00	0.00

FIGURE 7.7   Mega Ltd DD curve

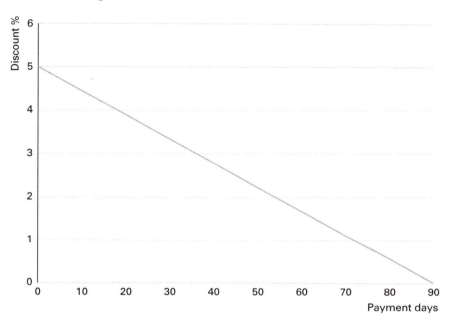

TABLE 7.17   Ultra Ltd discounting invoices on the system

Invoice no	PO no	Payment due date	Invoice value	Net invoice value
125	47500	10 days' time	$20,000	$19,888.89
154	47578	20 days' time	$25,000	$24,722.22
169	46001	40 days' time	$15,000	$14,666.67
179	46234	50 days' time	$25,000	$24,305.56
201	46645	60 days' time	$30,000	$29,000.00
Total			$115,000	$112,583.34

system, they will receive $112,583.34 and Mega Ltd will have a saving of $2,416.66 on their accounts payable. The system is dynamic, as the discount value of the invoices will change on a daily basis.

Enhancing procurement's value with data analytics

This section introduces data initiatives that are bridging the gap between the physical, information and financial flows, and increasing functional integration within an organization's intra- and inter-supply chain operation by adopting data analytics that process data into information.

Data can be generated and captured every time an interaction occurs whether it's a transaction between two businesses, a mobile phone call, your car's engine management system, a parcel being tracked along its journey, a visit to a company's website or purchases on your grocery loyalty card – many more examples exist. Next time you do your grocery shopping, look at your receipt and the valuable data that has been captured, which includes time, location, what you have bought, quantities, promotions and offers, how much you have spent, method of payment and loyalty points. When data is processed into information and communicated to the relevant decision maker its value appreciates. Combining different data sets can increase the value of the information, for example the synergies obtained from collecting transactional data from sales and marketing, and supplier and accounting transactions with your organization, to improve the visibility of managing customer returns.

There are three data analytics approaches that procurement practitioners can adopt that will enhance the impact of the decisions they take, improve the financial performance of their organization and increase their value to the organization: descriptive, predictive and prescriptive analytics. Each approach will be introduced below and their implications for procurement are highlighted.

Descriptive analytics

Descriptive analytics processes historical data to provide information that illuminates past events and highlights issues where an intervention is required. From a procurement perspective, examples include:

- product availability issues and stock outs;
- customer returns by stock-keeping unit (SKU);

- inventory mark-downs or write-offs by SKU;
- products returned to supplier;
- quality issues by SKU and supplier;
- product lead times;
- customer complaints.

The importance and value of this information is increased further if shared electronically with the organization's supplier base, who can then introduce corrective action based on the feedback generated by the descriptive analysis.

Predictive analytics

Predictive analytics uses historical data combined with statistical tools and techniques to analyse the data, searching for patterns, relationships and trends within the data that can be used to help predict future outcomes. This information would be extremely useful for procurement decisions; for example, if there was a positive relationship between the weather and product volumes, then information captured from weather forecasts could be used to place orders with suppliers. Analysing EPOS data can reveal an unexpected relationship between different product categories within a retail outlet, and provide opportunities to develop promotions or relocate them together to improve the customer's experience. The relationship between the time of day and the type of product purchased is extremely important information for procurement practitioners to ensure product availability and replenishment; for example the lunchtime meal deal, where three different items are bundled together.

Prescriptive analytics

Prescriptive analytics can be used to enhance procurement decisions by using data to develop simulation models, which can then be used to optimize future scenarios. A procurement decision to change the mode of transportation for the primary inbound distribution between a supplier based in Europe and the buyer in the UK from road freight to one based on intermodal using rail. The impact on cost, lead time, service levels, safety stock calculations, customer service and environmental factors would all need to be derived before making the decision to proceed with the change.

Summary and conclusions

Procurement decisions have a significant impact on the financial performance of an organization. They directly impact on the components (revenue and costs) of the income statement and in the balance sheet they affect the organization's total assets minus current liabilities. The ratios used to measure profitability, liquidity, working capital and efficiency are influenced by procurement decisions. The procurement function can reduce risk, improve financial sustainability and protect the organization's corporate reputation by adopting supplier relationship management, supplier audits and due diligence when dealing with suppliers. Harnessing the power of data analytics will enable procurement practitioners to create value for their organization and improve their strategic worth to the business.

References

Brookson, S (2001) *Understanding Accounts*, Dorling Kindersley, London

Christopher, M (2011) *Logistics and Supply Chain Management*, Prentice Hall, Harlow, Essex

CIMA (2005) *CIMA Official Terminology*, CIMA Publishing, Oxford

Deutsche Post DHL (2013) Annual Report 2013, https://www.dpdhl.com/content/dam/dpdhl/en/media-center/investors/documents/annual-reports/DPDHL_2013_Annual_Report.pdf (archived at https://perma.cc/Q45C-SCG9)

Deutsche Post DHL (2016) Annual Report 2016, https://www.dpdhl.com/en/investors/ir-download-center.html (archived at https://perma.cc/7QYY-RAXP)

Deutsche Post DHL (2018) Annual Report 2018, https://www.dpdhl.com/en/investors/ir-download-center.html (archived at https://perma.cc/7QYY-RAXP)

Deutsche Post DHL (2019) Annual Report 2019, https://www.dpdhl.com/en/investors/ir-download-center.html (archived at https://perma.cc/7QYY-RAXP)

Deutsche Post World Net (2007) Annual Report 2007, https://www.ipc.be/sector-data/reports-library/member-reports/deutsche-post-dhl/deutsche-post-2007 (archived at https://perma.cc/DN3L-9978)

Ellram, L M and Liu, B (2002) The financial impact of supply chain management, *Supply Chain Management Review*, **6** (6), pp 30–7

Euro Banking Association (2014) Supply Chain Finance: EBA European Market Guide, Version 2.0, June, https://www.abe-eba.eu/media/azure/production/1544/eba-market-guide-on-supply-chain-finance-version-20.pdf (archived at https://perma.cc/H64J-56N2)

Lukas, B A, Whitwell, G J and Doyle, P (2005) How can a shareholder value approach improve marketing's strategic influence? *Journal of Business Research*, **58** (4), pp 414–22

Porter, M (1985) *Competitive Advantage: Creating and sustaining superior performance*, Free Press, New York

Ryals, L and McDonald, M (2008) *Key Account Plans: The practitioners' guide to profitable planning*, Butterworth-Heinemann, Oxford

Templar, S C (2019) *Supply Chain Management Accounting*, Kogan Page, London

Templar, S C, Hofmann, E and Findlay, C (2016) *Financing The End-To-End Supply Chain: A reference guide to supply chain finance*, 1st edn, Kogan Page, London

Templar, S C, Hofmann, E and Findlay, C (2020) *Financing The End-To-End Supply Chain: A reference guide to supply chain finance*, 2nd edn, Kogan Page, London

Notes

1 See total cost of ownership

2 If you want to know more about the relationship between supply chain decisions and financial performance, see Templar (2019).

3 When calculating an organization's tax liability, different jurisdictions may have separate policies with regard to treating depreciation. Please check with your accounting department.

4 Total assets minus current liabilities equals capital employed.

5 Less than one year.

6 If you would like to know more about supply chain finance instruments, see Templar *et al* (2020).

08

Supply chain risk management

MARTIN CHRISTOPHER

In the opening months of 2020, the world became aware of a new coronavirus, COVID-19, and of the impact that it was having on global supply chains. Businesses in every sector and region were affected by factory shutdowns, travel restrictions and lockdowns. Supply shortages rapidly became apparent, often exacerbated by stockpiling both by companies and by consumers. The fragility of many organizations' supply networks was exposed and the knock-on effect on sales revenue and corporate profitability was profound. The scale of the impact of the pandemic on lives and livelihoods was immense. The economic ramifications have been enormous and the reverberations of this seismic event will be felt for many years to come.

Very few companies were prepared for this disruption. Paradoxically, in many countries where governments maintained the equivalent of a 'risk register' the threat of a pandemic was at the top of the list, or very close to the top.

What the COVID-19 crisis has highlighted is just how dependent every business has become on other entities in the supply chain. Indeed it has underlined the fact that these chains are not chains at all but complex interconnected networks. This is more than a semantic difference. In complex networks the nature and level of risk is different from the risk that exists in a simple, linear chain. 'Complexity' describes a condition of interconnectedness and interdependencies across a network where a change in one element can have an effect on other elements – often in unforeseen ways. Because so many of the interactions between agents and entities within a network can have a cumulative and combinatorial effect, the likelihood of disturbances and disruptions increases.

The more nodes and links that exist in a network, clearly the more complex it becomes. As a result of outsourcing non-core activities, many companies today are much more reliant on external suppliers of goods and services. These external suppliers are also dependent upon a web of second-tier suppliers and so on. There is a strong likelihood that the focal firm at the centre of the network will not even be aware of many of the second- or third-tier suppliers that feed their upstream supply chain. One example of good practice is provided by the agricultural equipment manufacturer, John Deere (see case study).

CASE STUDY
Managing upstream risk at John Deere

(One) way in which John Deere recognizes and manages complexity is through its supplier performance monitoring tool, which integrates traditional statistical process control approaches. Between 750 and 1,000 direct suppliers now are proactively monitored and managed by this monitoring tool. Specifically, a web environment was developed that asks suppliers a set of questions twice a year, covering an 18-month forecast period. Issues assessed include, for example, how comfortable the supplier feels with respect to second- and third-tier suppliers as well as any existing or projected capacity constraints. Deere's approach points to the importance of managing complexity in the supply network, not only at the tier-1 level but also at lower levels. With closely interconnected supply networks, coupled with just-in-time manufacturing and close-to-zero inventories, this deeper monitoring of suppliers is at the core of Deere's successful approach to managing complexity. The key activities are to proactively monitor capacity and the potential for supply disruption and impending disasters – and then to develop appropriate responses. Output reports are received every week. If there is a capacity issue, an action plan is developed to address the capacity shortages.

The system is constantly undergoing enhancements. To illustrate, in 2012, in order to increase compliance, Deere incorporated modules pertaining to a supplier's code of conduct and risk audit. One of the key issues addressed was restricted materials, such as conflict minerals. The objective is to automate searches for suppliers so that violations are immediately communicated and noticed. To achieve this objective, Deere held discussions with 69 of the most critical suppliers – on an executive-to-executive level – to identify whether they had business continuity planning and risk management approaches in place, and with their suppliers.

SOURCE Simhan *et al* (2013)

Understanding the risk profile

To enable managers to better understand the areas of potential vulnerability in their networks, a supply chain risk profile should be constructed. The purpose of the risk profile is to identify where the greatest threats to supply chain continuity lie and then to use this insight to develop risk mitigation strategies. Figure 8.1 highlights the four steps to building the profile.

FIGURE 8.1 Creating a supply chain risk profile

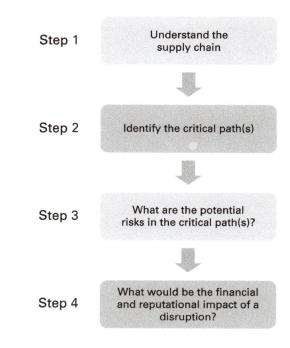

Let us examine each of these steps in turn.

1 Understand the supply chain

While it might seem obvious, a vital part of the supply chain risk management process is to understand the shape of the supply chain. In other words, we need to be able to map the network of which our business is a part. This map needs to cover all the nodes and links that together comprise the 'end-to-end' pipeline. In managing upstream supply risk, this implies our ability to look beyond the first-tier suppliers to gain an understanding of the second- and even third-tier supply base.

Clearly this is a challenging task, given the complexity of many supply chains. However, it can be done – as evidenced by companies bound by regulatory and compliance legislation to do just this, for example in pharmaceuticals, aerospace and certain food chains. New tools are now available to enable complex supply networks to be mapped. For example, so-called 'graph databases' can be used to search across networks to identify the interconnections between different networks, often exposing where potential 'pinch points' may lie. Organizations such as Sedex can assist in supply chain mapping by using shared information across their global membership. In this way upstream supply chains can be made transparent, and as a result a greater understanding of the nodes and links that constitute the company's supply network can be gained.

2 Identify the critical path(s)

In any supply network there will be some nodes and links that, if they were to fail, for whatever reason, the impact of that failure would be significant. What we should be looking for in building the risk profile for the businesses are those nodes and links that are 'mission critical' for the continued smooth running of the business. Of particular concern are those parts of the network where a disruption would have a severe impact on the company's profitability. Thus, a systematic review of the supply network should be conducted and for each node and link, the question is 'if this node or this link were to fail, what would be the effect on earnings?'

Those nodes and links where a failure would have the greatest impact might be thought of as forming the 'critical path' across the network.

Critical paths are likely to have a number of characteristics:

- Long lead times, for example the time taken to replenish a component from order to delivery.
- A single source of supply with no short-term alternative available.
- Where there are two or more first-tier suppliers who share the same second-tier supplier.
- Dependence on specific infrastructure, for example ports, transport modes or information systems.
- Bottlenecks or 'pinch points' through which material or product must flow.
- Nodes or links where a failure would take time to rectify.

One useful tool in the identification of critical paths is failure mode and effect analysis (FMEA) (McDermott *et al*, 2009). The purpose of FMEA is to provide a systematic approach to identifying where in a network attention should be focused to reduce the risk of failure. The idea is to look at each node and link and ask three questions:

- What could go wrong?
- What effect would this failure have?
- What are the key causes of this failure?

The next step is to assess potential failures in the network against the following criteria:

- What is the severity of the effect of failure?
- How likely is this failure to occur?
- How likely is the failure to be detected?

A rating system such as the one shown in Table 8.1 is then used to create a combined priority score by multiplying the three scores together.

TABLE 8.1 Failure mode and effect analysis (FMEA) rating system

S = Severity	1 No direct effect on operating service level
	2 Minor deterioration in operating service level
	3 Definite reduction in operating service level
	4 Serious deterioration in operating service level
	5 Operating service level approaches zero
O = Likelihood of occurrence	1 Probability of once in many years
	2 Probability of once in many operating months
	3 Probability of once in some operating weeks
	4 Probability of weekly occurrence
	5 Probability of daily occurrence
D = Likelihood of detection	1 Detectability is very high
	2 Considerable warning of failure before occurrence
	3 Some warning of failure before occurrence
	4 Little warning of failure before occurrence
	5 Detectability is effectively zero

3 What are the potential risks in the critical path(s)?

There are so many potential risks to the smooth running of any supply network and hence it is necessary to use some form of a systematic audit to help identify the most likely causes of disruption. This audit should examine the potential risk to business disruptions arising from five sources (see Table 8.2).

4 What would be the financial and reputational impact of a disruption?

The impact of supply chain disruptions on a business can be considerable. In extreme cases the severity of the disruption can lead to the collapse of the company. The effects of supply chain failures will often extend beyond the immediate short-term impact and can affect not only the bottom line but also the reputation of the business for some time into the future.

TABLE 8.2 The five sources of supply chain risk

1 Supply risk	How vulnerable is the business to disruptions in supply? Risk may be higher because of global sourcing, reliance on key suppliers, poor supply management, etc.
2 Demand risk	How volatile is demand? Does the 'bullwhip' effect cause demand amplification? Are there parallel interactions where the demand for another produce affects the demand for ours?
3 Process risk	How resilient are our processes? Do we understand the sources of variability in those processes? Where are the bottlenecks? How much additional capacity is available if required?
4 Control risk	How likely are disturbances and distortions to be caused by our own internal control systems? For example, order quantities, batch sizes and safety stock policies can distort demand signals.
5 Environmental risk	Which nodes and links might be particularly vulnerable to external forces, eg, weather-related events, earthquakes, geopolitical upheavals, regulations and compliance issues?

SOURCE Christopher (2011: 194)

One useful metric to employ when seeking to measure the financial effect of supply chain disruptions is 'cash flow at risk'. Essentially the idea is that for each of the critical paths previously identified there should be a regular 'stress test' conducted that seeks to understand what the impact of a failure would be on cash flow during the time it takes to rectify the problem.

Beyond 'cash flow at risk' is the wider – and potentially more damaging – question of 'reputational risk'. When in 2007 Mattel, the world's biggest toymaker, had to recall over 20 million toys because of potentially dangerous levels of lead in the paint used in the manufacture of those toys, the long-term impact on their reputation was considerable. It took several years before their sales recovered to previous levels. There are many other similar examples of the long-term impact of supply network disruptions.

While it is almost impossible to put a figure on the real cost of a loss of reputation in the marketplace, there is strong evidence that shareholder value is almost always adversely affected following a supply chain disruption (see for example, Singhal & Hendricks,

2002). Even though there may be no actual disruption to the supply chain, significant financial damage can be caused when events occur, which can have a lasting reputational effect. The case of British fashion retailer Boohoo (see case study) provides an example of how upstream ethical issues can have an impact on investor sentiment.

CASE STUDY
Reputational risk impacts market valuation

In the summer of 2020, the *Sunday Times* – a British newspaper – reported that undercover investigators had discovered that a UK-based supplier to Boohoo, a fast-growing fashion retailer, was paying its workers less than the legal minimum wage and was operating in unsafe conditions. While Boohoo denied any knowledge of what was happening at this supplier, investors responded with a widespread sell-off of their shares. Billions of pounds were wiped off Boohoo's market valuation as share prices fell. A major institutional investor, Aberdeen Standard Investments, one of the biggest shareholders in Boohoo, sold 27 million of its shares in the company – a sign that ethical concerns are increasingly driving investment decisions.

Creating a supplier risk profile

A common assumption in business is that supply chain risk arises primarily from external events over which the company has no control. Certainly there is always the potential for supply chains to be disrupted as a result of hurricanes, floods, labour disputes, pandemics, etc. However, much of the risk in supply chains today is there because of decisions that the organization itself has taken. In particular, sourcing and procurement decisions will be a major determinant of the risk profile of the business.

Ideally every decision that is taken on the choice of supplier should be shaped by asking the question: 'how is the risk profile impacted by this decision?' For example, if the decision is to source from a low-cost country at some distance from major markets, how will lead times be affected? What will be the impact on the ability of the business to respond to sudden changes in demand? Is there a greater risk of disruptive geopolitical events or regulatory change?

Too often sourcing decisions are made on a narrow definition of cost and do not always factor in the potential risk costs. When the risk profile is adversely impacted by sourcing decisions, the need for a higher level of supply chain governance will necessarily increase. Whereas in the past companies will often have monitored the financial health of their immediate suppliers they might not always have looked at the wider supply chain risk-related issues. In today's world of outsourced activities and 'leaned-down' supply chains, the procurement decision process has to be based on a full evaluation of the impact that sourcing choices have on the risk profile.

One immediate issue that arises as organizations seek to grapple with this challenge is that they often deal with hundreds, possibly thousands of suppliers. How can risk profiles be assessed given this level of complexity in the supply base? Also, as we have highlighted earlier, there are many potential sources of risk in the supply chain – some of which might impact some of our suppliers but not others. The way to handle this complexity is to broadly categorize both the supply base and the risk source to identify the priorities for more detailed analysis.

A useful categorization of the supply base that has been proposed (Giguere and Goldbach, 2012) is to classify suppliers in one of three types: strategic, tactical/core and transactional.

1 Strategic suppliers

As the name suggests, these suppliers are critical to the achievement of the company's business strategy. Without them it would potentially be very difficult for the organization to continue in business. It is likely that they will be few in number but their importance to the business is significant. They will be key sources of innovation, knowledge and other resources, and by working closely with them the focal firm can gain valuable differential advantage in the marketplace. With these suppliers the business will want to forge the strongest possible relationships at every level, from chief executive down to the factory floor. The emphasis will be on high levels of cross-boundary working, maximum transparency and creating a collaborative culture.

Because the business is so dependent for its own survival on these suppliers, it is vital that the focal firm understands their risk profiles just as well as their own and recognizes that any adverse changes to those profiles must be jointly addressed.

2 Tactical/core suppliers

The smooth day-to-day running of the business is greatly influenced by the performance of these 'tactical' or 'core' suppliers. They will be greater in number than the firm's strategic suppliers but still relatively few. These are the suppliers who, if they went out of business, would have a severe impact on the firm's operations at least on a temporary basis. However, they could be replaced and contingency plans should always be in place to cater for potential disruptions.

The likelihood is that these suppliers will account for a large proportion of the firm's total procurement spend. In addition, the focal firm will be relying on these suppliers to provide highly reliable performance – be it on-time delivery, operating and regulatory conformance or vendor-managed inventory programmes. For all these reasons it is critical that the business maintains a close monitor on any factors that are likely to impinge on these suppliers' ability to provide the requisite levels of cost, quality and delivery standards.

3 Transactional suppliers

The third category of suppliers might also be termed 'commodity' suppliers, in the sense that the products or services they supply are often widely available from alternative sources. Hence if, for whatever reason, one of these suppliers were unable to continue to supply the business it would not be difficult to find another supplier. Price is usually the primary consideration when making sourcing decisions for this category of supplier. Mechanisms such as e-auctions might be used to make the supplier search and selection process more cost-effective.

Because the likelihood is that these transactional suppliers will be more numerous than the other two categories, it is suggested that supplier risk monitoring be confined to some basic metrics, primarily to ensure that price and delivery performance remain competitive.

Having categorized the supply base in this way, the question remains as to what are the key dimensions of risk that need to be factored into the initial sourcing decisions, as well as the subsequent risk monitoring process.

One useful classification of risk types has been proposed by Favre and McCreery (2008). Their suggestion is that while there are many sources of risk, they can be grouped into three broad categories: industry/commodity risk; geographic risks; and environmental risks.

1 Industry/commodity risks

Some industries are more prone to certain types of supply chain risk and likewise some companies are more vulnerable to commodity risk in terms of price fluctuations, shortages, etc. In the food industry the impact of weather-related factors such as drought can have a major effect on availability and hence cost. Extreme weather conditions in Europe in recent years have led to a reduction in harvest yields of many crops. This has resulted in increased volatility in availability and hence prices. Many similar examples of weather-related disruptions are to be found in other regions and are expected to increase as the effects of climate change start to impact.

Other industry-specific risk sources in this category might relate to access to scarce materials, for example, rare earth metals or other scarce resources, such as trained and knowledgeable personnel.

In some industries, for example pharmaceuticals, regulatory change is a constant possibility, which can have far-reaching effects on business risk generally. The message here is that companies need to understand the particular threats that are specific to the industries of which they are a part, as well as the commodities upon which they depend.

2 Geographic risks

Because of the global nature of many of today's supply chains it is important that geographic risk assessment be part of the supply chain risk profiling process. Geographic risk can include political interventions, for example nationalization or terrorist or piracy activities, exchange rate fluctuations and input cost changes, for example labour. A number of specialist organizations now offer specific country risk profiles, which are regularly updated and focus particularly on potential sources of disruption.

One feature of geographic risk that is not so obvious relates to the likelihood that as a result of global sourcing, lead times will be extended and the number of border crossings may increase, as will the need for additional activities such as customs clearance.

As a result there will inevitably be an impact on the total amount of inventory both in the 'pipeline' and also additional safety stock that will be required to 'buffer' the company against the variability of supply. Longer lead times are almost always associated with greater variability, and greater variability means more inventory.

The risk dimension of inventory is not always fully appreciated. As well as the financial implications – how will the inventory be financed and at what cost? – there are the risks of obsolescence if market demand changes. Similarly, there are risks of increased out-of-stock situations if demand is greater than expected. The sum total of these inventory-related costs can be extremely high and can have a real impact on the profitability of the business and its return on investment.

3 Environmental risks

There are many potential sources of risk to supply chain continuity in the wider environment – mostly out of the control or influence of an individual business. Natural disasters such as floods, tsunamis, hurricanes, earthquakes and volcanoes can cause major disruption to the business, quite apart from their wider social and economic impact. Interestingly (or alarmingly, depending on your point of view), for whatever reason, these types of events seem to be on the increase. These risk sources may be low probability but often they are high impact in terms of their effect on supply chain operations.

As we have already highlighted earlier in this chapter, the impact of the global COVID-19 pandemic has had significant effects on almost every industrial sector.

While clearly external events of this variety cannot be forecast, to a certain extent they can be planned for and hence mitigated. Contingency planning is very much concerned with asking 'what if'-type questions and then conducting the equivalent of a 'stress test' to current supply chain arrangements. The idea of a stress test is that the business should seek to understand what would be the impact of, say, another volcanic ash cloud, originating in the northern hemisphere, upon our business? How well could the network cope with this disruption? Which would be the critical nodes and links that need to be reinforced or augmented?

Creating a supplier risk audit

Combining these two ideas we have introduced, that is, the type of supplier (strategic, tactical/core and transactional) and the risk categories (industry/commodity, geographical and environmental), enables us to create a basic framework to understand where our supply networks might be at greatest risk. Figure 8.2 outlines this framework.

The suggestion is that strategic suppliers should be audited regularly – certainly several times a year – to identify any changes to their risk profile. For tactical suppliers a less frequent review, say once a

FIGURE 8.2 Supply risk assessment framework

		RISK CATEGORY			
		Industry	Geography	Environment	
SUPPLIER CATEGORY	Strategic				Review regularly
	Tactical				Periodic review
	Transactional				Exception reporting

year, should suffice. Transactional suppliers, of whom there may be many, should be subject to automatic performance measurement (eg on-time delivery) and exceptions reported.

In this way, managing the risk assessment process across even a large supplier base becomes a feasible proposition. The end result of this systematic process should be a clearer view of where the main vulnerabilities exist among upstream suppliers.

The growing concern for cybersecurity

A common feature across all supply chains is their growing – sometimes total – reliance on information technology. Perhaps inevitably as supply chains become digital, it is disruptions to the flow of data and information that now pose one of the biggest threats to business continuity.

In recent years the prevalence of 'cyberattacks' has been on the increase. The source of these attacks is not always known and the motivation for the attack not always clear. The likelihood is that these attacks will continue to rise and that cyber-risk is likely to be the number one concern for business in the future. Sometimes this risk comes from the failure of internal IT systems, and a number of businesses have seen significant disruption from this source. British Airways in 2017 suffered a major IT system failure – with seemingly no back-up in place – that led to several days of cancellations, delays and severe negative customer reaction. However, many of the recent examples of breaches of cybersecurity have originated externally and have been designed with malicious intent. The impact on business performance of such orchestrated attacks can be considerable, as the case study below highlights.

CASE STUDY
Reckitt Benckiser hit by cyberattack

In July 2017 a number of major global businesses and government departments were severely affected by the 'NotPetya' cyberattack, which was thought to have originated in Ukraine. The attack spread by contagion through interlinked IT systems and across supply chains. One company hit by the attack was Reckitt Benckiser, one of the world's leading producers of fast-moving consumer goods. Some of their factories were closed for days as their planning systems failed, customer orders could not be processed and their enterprise planning systems were crippled.

It was estimated that the company lost £100 million ($137 million) of sales revenue as a result of the attack. Even though the company had previously recognized the possibility of such an attack and had reviewed its cybersecurity systems, it still proved vulnerable to this new source of supply chain risk.

There is a growing concern that cyber-risk may enter through the 'back door' of the business – meaning that the entry point for malware-type attacks can be through suppliers. The implication of this possibility is that the procurement and supply management function must be cognizant of these potential issues and become much more concerned with ensuring that supplier partnerships are safeguarded by robust firewalls to reduce or eliminate the possibility of cyber-risk contagion.

Creating a more resilient supply chain

No matter how rigorous the risk assessment process is, there will always be things that go wrong in any supply chain. Disruptions and unexpected events are inevitable in even the best-run business. Because of this it is important that supply chains are designed with resilience in mind. Resilience implies the ability of a system to return to its original or desired state after being disturbed (Cranfield School of Management, 2003).

There are a number of basic building blocks that must be put in place to create the foundations for a more resilient supply chain. Figure 8.3 summarizes the key elements.

FIGURE 8.3 Creating a resilient supply chain

Let us consider each of these four elements in turn:

1 Supply chain (re-)engineering

The actual design of the supply chain will have a major effect on its resilience. Often supply chain networks are designed to optimize cost. While the economic logic behind this idea is strong, it may be that a network optimized on cost is not the most resilient. Low-cost country sourcing, lean manufacturing and centralized distribution centres are examples of supply chain decisions that may reduce costs but which may not enhance resilience.

Organizations seeking to create a more resilient supply network should begin with seeking to map their existing arrangements – a step we term 'supply chain understanding'. Essentially the purpose of the supply chain map is to determine the 'as is' status of the supply network, looking for specific bottlenecks or 'pinch points' and identifying opportunities for re-engineering the system to remove unnecessary complexity. It is particularly important to extend the map as far upstream as possible into second- or even third-tier suppliers to look for critical suppliers

FIGURE 8.4 Looking upstream for critical suppliers

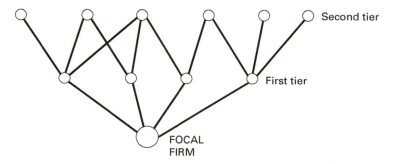

who may be hidden from view. An example would be as shown in Figure 8.4, where three first-tier suppliers share the same second-tier supplier. If that second-tier supplier were to fail, it could be the cause of a major disruption to the supply chain.

Hopefully, resulting from this detailed mapping of the upstream supply network there will be a clearer understanding of the potential vulnerabilities facing the business. The question now becomes one of determining how best to build resilience into the network. One way to achieve resilience is through redundancy, that is, by deliberately creating 'slack' along the critical paths perhaps by increasing capacity, or by duplicating certain nodes and links. While a certain amount of redundancy may be desirable, a more attractive solution might be to work with critical suppliers to introduce a higher level of contingency planning. For example, the French car company PSA Peugeot Citroën has implemented a policy whereby all its suppliers have to have alternative sources of supply in different countries. This policy of dual sourcing in different geographies was introduced following disruptions caused by an earthquake in Japan in 2011.

Supply chain resilience essentially requires the existence of buffers to act as 'shock absorbers'. Typically, these buffers are provided by inventory, capacity or lead times. All of these mechanisms will involve a cost, which should be viewed as insurance against the costs of disruption. Using inventory as a buffer may be controversial in a world where 'just-in-time' and 'zero inventory' strategies have been widely adopted. However, holding strategic inventory, preferably in a generic form, at certain locations in the network can provide a significant shock-absorbing capacity. Likewise having access to additional capacity when required can also provide much needed 'headroom'. That capacity need not be owned by the business but could be paid for as and when required. Finally, there may be an opportunity to use time as a buffer – not by making the customer wait longer but by reducing non-value-adding time in a process and keeping the time saved to be used 'just-in-case'.

Designing supply chains with the objective of enhancing resilience should be standard practice in today's volatile world. Indeed, the basis for all supply chain design should be the principle that the best decisions are those decisions that keep the most options open. In reality, many supply chain decisions are taken purely with cost reduction in mind and rarely factor in the impact of those decisions on risk profiles and resilience.

2 Supply chain collaboration

Even though much has been written and spoken about the need for a higher level of collaborative working across the supply chain, it still tends to be the exception rather than the rule. Nevertheless, if the objective is to create a more resilient supply chain then supply chain collaboration has to be a prerequisite.

Collaboration is essential to ensuring visibility across the supply chain. Without the ability to see clearly upstream and downstream, uncertainty will increase and the ability to respond to events will be impaired. Tools such as supply chain event management (SCEM), which enable critical stages in the supply chain to be monitored to check for deviations from the plan, can be effective only if there is a willingness among supply chain partners to share information. A beneficial spin-off from shared information between partners is a likely reduction in 'bullwhips' where disturbances are magnified because of a lack of visibility (Christopher and Lee, 2004). Collaborative planning can also enable a transition away from order-triggered replenishment to some form of vendor-managed inventory (VMI). Implementing VMI, whereby suppliers automatically replenish their customers' inventory, can significantly reduce the total amount of safety stock in the system as well as improving forecast accuracy, since suppliers can see further down the pipeline.

A further benefit of closer collaboration is that supply chain 'intelligence' can be vastly enhanced if the key players in a supply chain are prepared to sit down together to pool their knowledge and insights. Ideally the business should establish a 'supply chain council' of key tier-1 suppliers that meets regularly to review risk profiles and to explore opportunities for further integration by working more closely across organizational boundaries.

3 Building a supply chain risk management culture

Several decades ago, when the idea of total quality management (TQM) began to take hold in many companies, it was quickly recognized that to make it work required the establishment of a culture of quality across the organization. The same can be said to be true of supply chain resilience. If organizations are to be better prepared for supply chain disruptions then risk management must be embedded in the corporate DNA. For this to happen, the board must make supply resilience a business priority. The chief procurement officer (CPO) should take the lead in developing a broad-based programme for ensuring that supply chain risk is taken seriously at all levels of the organization. Thus, every decision that is taken, be it at board level or on the shop floor, should be subject to the question: 'What will be the likely effect of this decision on the risk profile of the business and will it affect our resilience?' Employees and managers should be encouraged to report their concerns about potential risks and also their ideas on how those risks could be mitigated.

Some years ago, business continuity planning (BCP) was adopted by many companies as a way to assess operational risk and to establish contingency arrangements. It can be argued now that the idea of BCP should be broadened and extended to become 'supply chain continuity planning'.

Continuity planning in a supply chain context should extend beyond the boundaries of individual businesses in the network and should seek to identify how the system as a whole should respond to a disturbance to the system. To help make this possible a supply chain continuity team should be established, reporting directly to the CPO.

The purpose of the team is to constantly review the risk profiles of suppliers, evaluate the current status of potential 'pinch points' in the supply chain (eg ports, transport links, infrastructure, etc), and to use this information to compile and update a 'risk register'. The membership of the team should encompass all the key players engaged in the procurement-to-delivery process.

4 Developing agile and adaptive capabilities

Almost certainly, achieving a more resilient supply chain will not be possible unless there is an emphasis on making the supply chain more agile and responsive. Clearly if organizations and systems are too slow to respond to a disturbance or disruption they are at a disadvantage when unexpected events happen. Agility in effect determines the firm's ability to move quickly when required. However, just as important as agility is adaptability.

Adaptability implies that if the environment changes, the supply chain can change to meet the new requirements. A problem for many companies is that they lack the flexibility to quickly change the shape of the supply network. Because these businesses typically have invested in 'bricks and mortar' and probably have little flexibility in their supply arrangements, they are unable to change the 'architecture' of their supply chain in the short term. An alternative idea that has been suggested (Christopher and Holweg, 2011) is that businesses should invest in acquiring *structural flexibility*. Essentially this approach suggests that owning assets and being locked in to existing supply arrangements and distribution channels might be disadvantageous in a fast-changing world. Thus resilience, it can be argued, is enhanced by seeking to shift the emphasis in procurement away from a cost-based approach towards a sourcing strategy that has the objective of maximizing flexibility. Clearly this is a perspective that might not find much support as companies seek to squeeze out costs and constantly seek to improve efficiencies. Nevertheless, the likelihood is that those companies that place the priority on investing in capabilities to enable a quicker response to unexpected changes and disruptions will outlast their cost-focused competitors.

Summary and conclusions

In this chapter we have highlighted the challenges that face companies resulting from higher levels of supply chain vulnerability. It should be emphasized, however, that there can be an 'upside' to risk as well as a 'downside'. For those companies that are prepared to embrace uncertainty and change and to invest in the capabilities to become more resilient, there are significant opportunities. In the words of Charles Darwin: 'It is not the strongest of the species that survives nor the most intelligent, but the one most responsive to change.'

References

Christopher, M (2011) *Logistics and Supply Chain Management,* Prentice Hall, Harlow

Christopher, M and Holweg, M (2011) Supply chain 2.0: managing supply chains in the age of turbulence, *International Journal of Physical Distribution and Logistics Management,* **41** (1), pp 63–82

Christopher, M and Lee, H (2004) Mitigating supply chain risk through improved confidence, *International Journal of Physical Distribution and Logistics Management,* **34** (5), pp 388–96

Cranfield School of Management (2003) *Creating Resilient Supply Chains: A practical Guide*, Centre for Logistics and Supply Chain Management, Cranfield University, UK

Favre, D and McCreery, J (2008) Coming to grips with supplier risk, *Supply Chain Management Review*, September

Giguere, M and Goldbach, G (2012) Segment your suppliers to reduce risk, *Supply Chain Quarterly*, **3**, pp 26–30

McDermott, R E, Mikulak, R J and Beauregard, M R (2009) *The basics of FMEA*, 2nd edn, Productivity Press, New York, NY

Simhan, N, Schoenherr, T and Sandor, J (2013) Profiles in Supply Management, *Supply Chain Management Review*, July/August, pp 10–13

Singhal, V R and Hendricks, K (2002) How supply chain glitches torpedo shareholder value, *Supply Chain Management Review*, January/February

09

Digitization of procurement

The enabling role of technology

REMKO VAN HOEK

Technology plays a key role in the maturation of the procurement profession and function. Technology has enabled more efficient and easier to use procurement processes, while freeing up bandwidth in the procurement team to focus on business partnering and strategic issues, internally and with suppliers. Looking into the future, further digitization opportunities exist and newer technologies and applications can be considered. In addition to careful consideration of these technologies, their impact on talent requirements for the procurement team also need to be considered.

Levels of automation and the role of technology in the procurement journey

Technology plays a key role in the maturation of procurement. The automation and streamlining of the ordering cycle frees up a lot of bandwidth in the procurement team to focus more on strategic sourcing. Essentially, technology reduces the need for teams to process purchase orders and firefight ordering issues. Creating a user-friendly ordering cycle system also drives adoption of procurement agreements and compliance with the procurement process. Put simply, if the system does not work or is complex to use, people may just work around the procurement process. This in turn reduces visibility of spend needed as input for strategic sourcing and supplier relationship management (SRM).

Technology in the sourcing process can help drive the productivity of the procurement team as well as bring better business intelligence from spend analysis into the sourcing process. The latter in particular can enhance the ability of procurement teams to drive the development of sourcing strategies. Automation of tendering and negotiating can not only drive productivity, but also grow the effectiveness of these sourcing steps; competition may increase among suppliers and more suppliers may be engaged in the tender process.

In the SRM process, technology can facilitate supplier engagement and performance evaluation. Just as it is common for sales teams to use customer relationship management (CRM) tools, procurement may do the same. A shared repository of information about key suppliers and the company's interactions with them can enable SRM effectiveness. A tool that can also be used for dashboarding and relationship governance may be shared with suppliers to move part of the ongoing relationship management efforts online and establish a single, joint version of the truth.

Figure 9.1 is from a study by the Hackett Group and it reports on levels of automation across the core procurement processes. The greatest levels of automation are reported in the ordering cycle (payments, accounts payable, procurement operations) and spend analysis. Beyond spend analysis (part of the sourcing process), the strategic sourcing process and SRM are less widely automated. This implies that technology may enable still further maturation of the procurement function today. The next section will review examples of technology applications in procurement, and then we will cover specific areas of procurement technology application.

FIGURE 9.1 Automation levels by procurement area

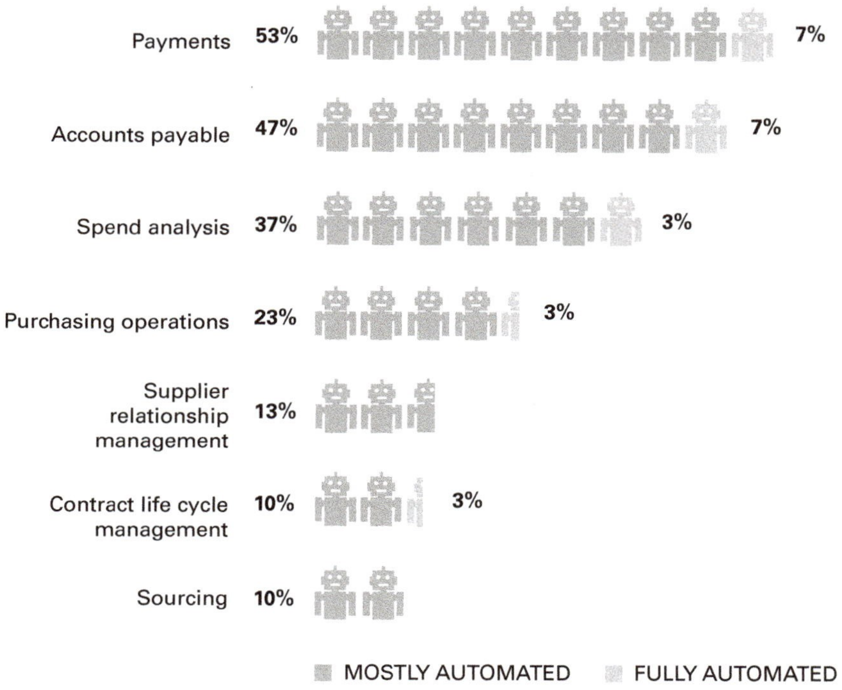

Payments	**53%**	**7%**
Accounts payable	**47%**	**7%**
Spend analysis	**37%**	**3%**
Purchasing operations	**23%**	**3%**
Supplier relationship management	**13%**	
Contract life cycle management	**10%**	**3%**
Sourcing	**10%**	

■ MOSTLY AUTOMATED   ■ FULLY AUTOMATED

SOURCE The Hackett Group

CASE STUDY

Vodafone procurement digitization

Traditional challenges in procurement include the lack of comprehensive, close to real time, data about external spend and procurement processes. How much are we spending with this supplier? How many businesses work with this supplier? Are all the orders going through the ordering cycle? What are the savings we are achieving for this business unit? How reliable are the supplier's deliveries? At Vodafone the procurement team has decided to digitize and automate part of its process in order to solve these challenges. 'It was frustrating how many dashboards we ran in Excel. And the biggest challenge was that it took weeks to get the data collected, cleaned up and the report built. By the time we were reviewing with the business, the data was already outdated and not that helpful anymore,' says Ninian Wilson, head of procurement at Vodafone.

Vodafone has 23 business units that are supported by a procurement team of 250 in their central procurement operation in Luxembourg and by 400 buyers located in the various businesses and regions. The team is responsible for €20 billion in annual spend across 800,000 purchase orders and 5 million invoices per year. The four main areas of spend are IT, network, services and devices.

Digitization started in the ordering cycle, then moved into strategic sourcing and SRM, and impacted engagement with the board, business unit leaders and within the procurement team. The value of digitization includes:

- more timely information that informs more meaningful discussion and decision making;
- greater service and faster support to procurement's internal customers in the business; higher productivity in procurement; and
- greater adoption of procurement processes and supplier contracts.

Perhaps most excitingly, the digital tools drive engagement in procurement in the business and company leadership and are fun and exciting for the procurement team.

Initially the team automated its performance and spend dashboard. The dashboard included a full set of metrics about key supply chain topics, including health and safety records, savings and working capital. Across an initial project of nine months, a newly formed team of data scientists and data analytics experts built a control centre, fed with 20 terabytes of data and three years' worth of transactions. It uses visualization tools that allow users to customize views, dig into data and approach the data from different angles, such as by business, geography or user. Example metrics include:

- the use of procurement catalogues;
- the time it takes to process purchase orders;
- the time to purchase order approval;
- the percentage of purchase orders that need rework.

This last metric has gone down from 28 per cent to 5 per cent and herein lies the key. By making the ordering cycle more efficient and reliable it frees up a lot of time for the procurement team to focus on strategic sourcing, instead of on firefighting and chasing purchase orders. The ease of use also drives adoption and compliance with the procurement process.

FIGURE 9.2 KPIs

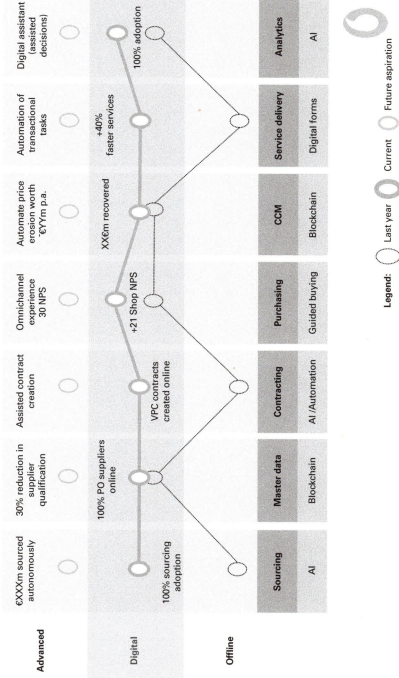

The control centre is now used to inform strategic sourcing efforts. Better spend data makes it easier to consider who from the business to involve, and the procurement team can bring better intelligence to its interactions with the business. This makes it easier for the procurement team to assume its role as a business partner. The discussion can focus on the development of sourcing strategies, not on the reliability and accuracy of spend data.

The next chapter in Vodafone's digital journey was automating some of its strategic sourcing process. When requests for procurement support come in from the business, they can be assigned to teams based upon category and business expertise, as well as team capacity. Fully autonomous procurement for some areas of spend is next on the horizon. This will enable speed of response and improve user experience. Think of it as DIY procurement. For example, the tool lets business users develop a request for proposal (RFP) by pulling questions from a bank of recommended questions. Procurement ensures that minimum standards for the sourcing process become a requirement for the release of the RFP, but it does not have to 'reinvent the wheel' for every new sourcing project.

A further step forward is the development of supplier relationship dashboards for executives. This will bring the same intelligence approach to the SRM process. Executives will be able to get an up-to-date snapshot of the status of the relationship and will be able to drill down into improvement opportunities for their engagement with suppliers. By allowing suppliers to input part of the data, a joint view of the status is achieved, reducing the need to 'compare notes' and creating a shared single version of the truth.

> The quality and granularity of data, the speed of execution, the ease of use and the ability to focus on strategy not data collection, all of this has elevated the business value of procurement. The operational effectiveness of procurement has improved with a factor 2 in just 3 years. Not only has digitization created new roles and tools, it has also elevated to contribution and impact of the procurement team members (Ninian Wilson).

Digitization application areas and benefits

There are plenty of technology options dedicated to and available in procurement, and for most technologies there are multiple competing providers. In the future, the technology landscape will evolve with newer technologies entering the procurement space, and this section will explore some of those.

1 Technologies in the ordering cycle

Part of the reason why automation levels are highest in the ordering cycle is that automating this process enables sourcing teams to focus more on strategic sourcing and being business partners, instead of purchase order processors. Additionally, it is common for the ordering cycle to be embedded in a finance enterprise resource planning (ERP) system; this makes it part of a core enterprise information technology architecture that does not benefit only procurement objectives. The case for investment in automating the ordering cycle can also be made from an accounting, controlling and financial management perspective.

ORDERING IN ERP

Typically the purchase order process is automated in ERPs, such as those offered by SAP, Oracle and Workday, by creating an opportunity for business people from outside of procurement to enter purchase order (PO) requests. These can go through an automated approval process that typically involves budget holders, with more and higher-up sign-offs required as the spend level of the PO goes up. In addition to the budget holder, there may be finance and procurement authorizations involved. When all authorizations are received the system can generate a PO and send it to the supplier of choice. Typically, this PO will include a dedicated number to be referenced on the invoice, a reference to standard terms and conditions, and specification of delivery instructions (by when, to whom, and where). The key benefits of this technology include less time spent on administrative tasks, ensuring proper up front authorization of spend and the use of a single buying process, as well as the ability to track spend and check invoices against POs in order to ensure that invoices are actually for goods and services needed and ordered. Essentially a PO is a 'mini contract'; it commits the company externally to supplying specified goods and services and articulates the terms for doing so.

VENDOR PORTAL AND VENDOR MASTER

A vendor portal can be used for suppliers to register on the company's vendor master. Registering on such a portal, often an extension of a finance ERP system, is fairly easy and involves the creation of a vendor record, with contact details and acceptance of terms of business. The benefit of this technology is that some of the administration is handled by the supplier and that records can be updated more easily. The vendor master is used to pull the supplier details used to generate a PO. The vendor master also provides a line of sight into how many suppliers the company is using; this number is often much higher than expected.

CATALOGUES AND ORDERING PORTALS

Because companies typically work with many suppliers, the use of catalogues is common and a great way to make procurement more 'hands-free' and user friendly. By developing catalogues or establishing access to online catalogues such as Amazon for Business or Staples.com, the number of POs for small purchase amounts can be much reduced. As a form of demand management, the assortment in the catalogues can be managed and access to the ordering function can be managed across the organization. Ordering portals can also be developed for travel (Egencia, for example) or office equipment. Both HP and Dell, for example, will develop ordering portals for B2B customers with the agreed-upon assortment and pricing available for ordering. These vendors can then invoice by order or even aggregate orders into monthly invoices. For smaller purchases in particular (office supplies, gifts), this can reduce the number of suppliers to maintain and the number of POs and payments to process. In addition to this efficiency, procurement can ensure that demand is met within company policy and agreed-upon pricing and product ranges. Users in the business experience an easier-to-navigate procurement process for smaller and standard purchases.

2 Technologies in the sourcing process

Spend analysis tools are the most widely used technology in the sourcing process. As an extension of the ERP used in the ordering cycle, spend analytics can automate the development of a spend cube and achieve more real-time data about spend with suppliers, by business unit, budget area and budget holder. These can provide a meaningful starting point for scoping strategic sourcing projects as discussed in Chapter 3. The spend cube helps identify who main spenders and stakeholders in the business are, and provides a great basis for reflecting upon current spending (number of suppliers, overlap of suppliers, growth of spend, etc). The benefit of automating spend analysis is a reduced reliance on manual spreadsheets and the ability to focus on interpreting the data instead of the accuracy and timeliness of data.

E-SOURCING

To automate steps after spend analysis in the strategic sourcing process, e-sourcing suites can be used. These workflow tools provide the option to develop tender documents, receive supplier proposals and evaluate suppliers. The tool can be used by the multifunctional tender team and tender documents can be shared electronically with suppliers. Suppliers in turn can respond to the tenders online. The benefit of this workflow automation is productivity of the tender team; the team does not have to compile a comparison of suppliers or input supplier proposals. Access can be distributed across the team and there is only one version of each of the main documents used during the process. Several of the major ERP companies have acquired e-sourcing software companies as an extension of their offering, beyond the ordering cycle. SAP bought Ariba and Workday purchased Scout RFP, for example.

E-AUCTIONS

A more tactical tool that can be used in the strategic sourcing process is e-auctions. These portals put the bidding process, typically part of the negotiations stage, after initial supplier qualification and evaluation, in a dynamic, real-time online setting. The suppliers essentially have a time window in which to enter bids, and they can see if their bid is in a winning position versus the competing bids. Because all suppliers can bid, the competitive pressure tends to accelerate the negotiations process and can improve the negotiation outcomes. Obviously, the use of e-auctions needs to be considered in the context of the sourcing strategy. It is more relevant for price-centric sourcing strategies and may not apply to all types of products and supplier segments. While catalogues may be used for routine suppliers, for leverage suppliers e-auctions may be beneficial. For bottleneck and strategic suppliers, the focus may be more on value-centric strategies instead.

3 Technologies in the SRM process

CONTRACT MANAGEMENT

As procurement organizations mature, the number of supplier contracts and agreements grow, and the use of contract management tools becomes a valuable consideration. By building a digital repository that is shared in the organization, contracts cannot get lost and are easier to find. Adding in alerts about upcoming renewals, price updates and major supplier meetings can ensure proactive management of the contracts by the procurement team.

SUPPLIER GOVERNANCE AND PERFORMANCE PORTAL

In addition to supplier registration and online ordering, companies may also establish a supplier portal that can be used to exchange performance information and keep track of improvement action items, upcoming meetings and key stakeholders in the relationship. All of these enable SRM efforts and create more enterprise-to-enterprise visibility and a shared version of the truth and agenda of action items.

Focus for the future: analytics and new technologies

While the technologies overviewed in the last section are well known and widely considered, more work remains to be done. Figure 9.3 shows how procurement executives see a lot of added impact potential in strategic sourcing and order cycle tools, as well as ERP (bars 2–4 from the top). They are also seeing a large focus on improving analytics and considering newer technologies such as robotics, digital apps and IoT. Blockchain is also considered, as the Walmart case study illustrates.

FIGURE 9.3 Greatest technology impact areas in the coming years

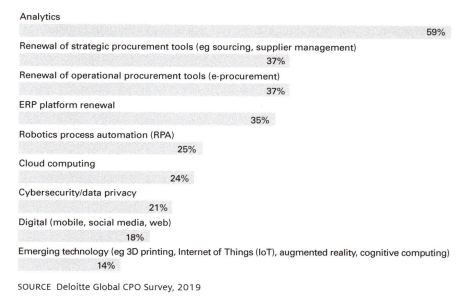

Analytics
59%

Renewal of strategic procurement tools (eg sourcing, supplier management)
37%

Renewal of operational procurement tools (e-procurement)
37%

ERP platform renewal
35%

Robotics process automation (RPA)
25%

Cloud computing
24%

Cybersecurity/data privacy
21%

Digital (mobile, social media, web)
18%

Emerging technology (eg 3D printing, Internet of Things (IoT), augmented reality, cognitive computing)
14%

SOURCE Deloitte Global CPO Survey, 2019

CASE STUDY

Walmart blockchain

Walmart has introduced blockchain in its relationships with over 100 green leaf
suppliers (lettuce, etc) in the United States. The application of blockchain
enables the company to trace individual product from the shelves in a store back
to the farm that the product came from in seconds, because all product is
individually tagged on the blockchain, as are the steps in the delivery process.
Based upon this traceability, if there is an issue with a product this can be
addressed with laser target at the source very quickly. This replaces the need to
empty all the shelves while the source of the food safety issue is traced back
upstream in the supply chain, as was done in the past, over a number of days. In
that situation there was a lot more food waste, economic loss and consumer
fear, whereas now the issue can be traced back to the source fast and accurately.
Walmart is also using blockchain to verify product authenticity back to the
source in China and to verify deliveries are made against shipment invoices.

Newer technologies such as robotics and blockchain need to be considered and evaluated for their potential value. The process of consideration to implementation of technology may include a few steps, including use case development, pilot and proof of concept, larger-scale roll-out, ongoing maintenance and updating, with evaluations taking place after each of those steps. Figure 9.4 offers evaluation criteria for newer technologies and pilot design suggestions, based on Verhoeven *et al* (2018) and van Hoek (2019a):

- Contribution of the technology to supply chain objectives.

- Engagement with the technology: are the technological features named clearly?

- Technological novelty seeking: is there reasoning for the necessity of blockchain technology or can the business problem be solved with an existing technology?

- Awareness of local context: how specifically will the use case fit into the supply chain context?

- Cognizance of alternative technologies: are alternatives considered?

- Anticipation of technology alteration: are use cases adaptable?

Of these criteria the first one is likely the single most important consideration. By considering what problem a technology may help solve, the risk of 'a solution looking for a problem' or 'technology push' can be reduced and we can ensure that we are approaching technology with the correct mindset, that is, as an enabler but not as a purpose in and of itself. With these evaluation criteria, the design of a pilot needs to factor in how specifically the technology can impact supply chain objectives, and who the executives and key stakeholders to involve are, and a pilot can be targeted as a result. Cognizance of alternative technologies is relevant for most procurement technologies, as companies typically use several technologies and tools already. Blockchain, for example, may use data feeds from RFID and bar codes, and link to the ordering cycle in ERP.

FIGURE 9.4 Criteria for evaluating technology

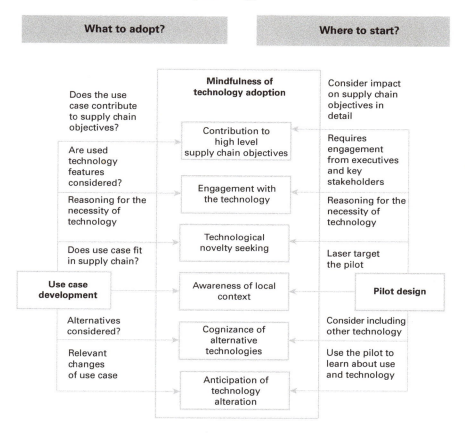

A further set of implementation considerations is offered in Figure 9.5, based on van Hoek (2019b). Drivers include internal and external considerations; in the procurement space this can include internal savings targets or external supply risks. Leadership and stakeholder commitment in procurement technology implementation is just as important as it is in the strategic sourcing and SRM process, and the alignment methods covered in Chapter 2 may be used to ensure commitment. Several barriers to implementation can be avoided by screening use cases and pilots through the criteria in Figure 9.4, but training may also be needed and the next section will revisit this.

FIGURE 9.5 Technology implementation considerations in the supply chain

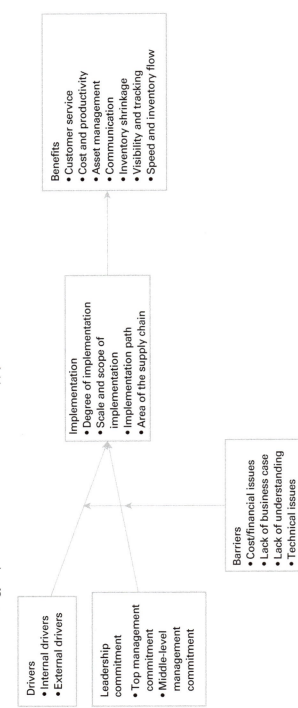

To scope and phase implementation, companies may move from a small pilot to gradual roll-out across procurement's typically comprehensive stakeholder landscape. Benefits tie back to the supply chain objectives that fundamentally underpin a use case and those reviewed in the overview of procurement technologies.

Impact on talent

With a major focus on furthering digitization, in analytics in particular, a key question is how to achieve this. Figure 9.6 offers action steps that the Hackett group found in its survey. Note that at the very top are two basics: improving data quality and master data management. This is a useful reminder that even with advanced technologies the basics still need to be focused on in order to avoid the use of advanced technologies on poor data sets. Beyond that, training and hiring new talent are listed. For training specifically, Figure 9.7 shows

FIGURE 9.6 Steps procurement managers are taking to advance analytics

Improve data quality and accessibility	55%
Improve master data management	50%
Enable self-service analytics	47%
Train existing talent on data analytics	45%
Invest in and deploy advanced analytics technologies (eg machine learning, data visualization)	39%
Hire data analytics talent in procurement	29%
Establish analytics centre of excellence	26%
Create data architecture suitable for structured and unstructured data	16%
Support hiring data analytics talent in business functions	16%

SOURCE Key Issues Study, The Hackett Group, 2020

FIGURE 9.7 Training areas in digital procurement

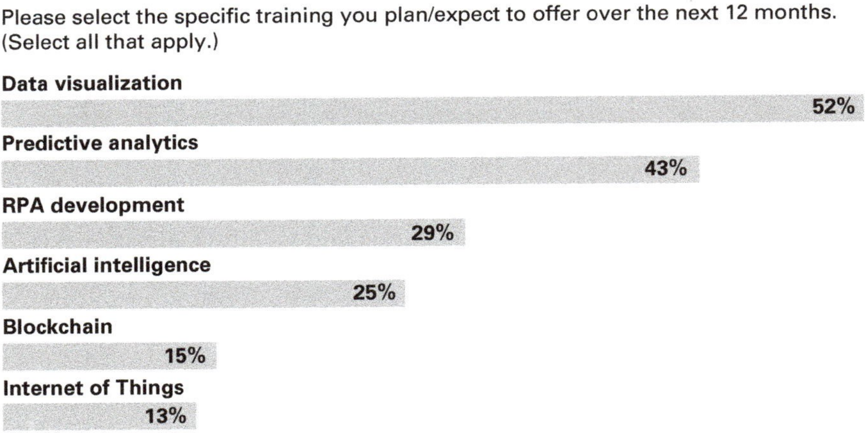

Please select the specific training you plan/expect to offer over the next 12 months.
(Select all that apply.)

Data visualization

52%

Predictive analytics

43%

RPA development

29%

Artificial intelligence

25%

Blockchain

15%

Internet of Things

13%

SOURCE Deloitte Global CPO Survey, 2019

TABLE 9.1 Top 10 current and future competencies in procurement

Current Competencies	Current Competencies
Analytical skills	Analytical skills
Basic knowledge on PSM role & processes	Automation
Communication skills	Big Data Analytics
Cross-functional abilities & knowledge	Computer Literacy
Interpersonal communication	eProcurement Technology
Negotiation	Holistic supply chain thinking
Stakeholder relationship management	Process optimization
Strategic sourcing	Strategic sourcing
Strategic thinking	Strategic thinking
Sustainability	Sustainability

SOURCE Bals *et al* (2019)

the training areas focused on, according to Deloitte. The figure implies a balance between learning about technologies such as blockchain itself, and usage training in visualization and analysis. The latter appears more important.

The investment in this training impacts the future competencies in the procurement function and Bals *et al* (2019) found, as shown in Table 9.1, that automation, big data and computer literacy are on the rise, while a focus on strategic sourcing remains. As a result, students of procurement and procurement professionals are well advised to invest in learning in this space as it will likely increase the market currency of their skill set.

Summary and conclusions

Technology has played a key role in the maturation of procurement and will continue to do so. Companies are both rolling out further technologies in core procurement processes, as well as considering newer technologies such as blockchain and robotics. It should be noted, however, that technology is an enabler and not a purpose in and of itself. A first question in considering technology is what supply chain problem it will resolve; this will help reduce the risk of 'technology push'. For the implementation of technology in procurement, some training in the use of the technology may be needed, and ensuring the right stakeholder involvement and training may be more important for a successful implementation than the technology itself. As procurement further digitizes the competency requirements for procurement professionals, it will continue to evolve towards the use of big data and automation in addition to existing requirements such as strategic sourcing and strategic thinking.

References

Bals, L, Schulze, H, Kelly, S and Stek, K (2019) Purchasing and supply management (PSM) competencies: current and future requirements, *Journal of Purchasing and Supply Management*, **25** (5)

van Hoek, R (2019a) Developing a framework for considering blockchain pilots in the supply chain – lessons from early industry adopters, *Supply Chain Management*, **25** (1), pp 115–21 van Hoek, R (2019b) Exploring blockchain implementation in the supply chain: learning from pioneers and RFID research, *International Journal of Operations & Production Management*, **39** (6/7/8), pp 829–59

Verhoeven, P, Sinn, F and Herden, T T (2018) Examples from blockchain implementations in logistics and supply chain management: exploring the mindful use of a new technology, *Logistics*, **2** (3): 20

PART FOUR

Sustaining procurement performance

10

Sustainable procurement

CARLOS MENA

The concept of sustainable development has received increasing attention from the business community over the last couple of decades. The concept was first popularized by the Brundtland Commission of the United Nations, which defined it as 'development that meets the needs of the present without compromising the ability of future generations to meet their own needs' (UN, 1987). In 2000 the UN moved the agenda forward with the development of the Global Compact, a set of principles that support sustainable development and acknowledge the role of the private sector (UN, 2020). The Global Compact covers the areas of human rights, labour, environment and anti-corruption. More recently, the Global Compact was updated with a specific set of benchmarks (see case study) (UN, 2020).

Three dimensions of sustainable development, known as the 'triple bottom line' (3BL), are often considered: economic, social and environmental. Traditionally procurement professionals have focused mainly on the economic ramifications of their decisions. However, the sustainability perspective has brought increasing attention to social and environmental aspects. For many, this has meant acknowledging that the impact of their organizations on society and the environment is not limited by its own four walls but stretches across the entire supply chain (Lamming and Hampson, 1996). Figure 10.1 presents the 3BL model and highlights some of the critical issues for procurement.

FIGURE 10.1   The triple bottom line: key issues in procurement

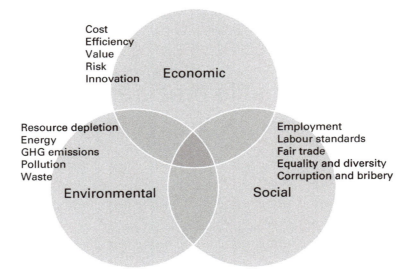

So far, the book has focused on the economic aspects of procurement. This chapter concentrates on the environmental and social aspects. We present the factors that are driving sustainable procurement and the barriers and challenges in its implementation. Finally, we discuss how sustainability fits in the process of strategic procurement and the tools that can be used to support it.

CASE STUDY
The UN Global Compact 10 principles

The UN Global Compact asks companies to embrace, support and enact, within their sphere of influence, a set of core values across four areas:

- Human Rights
    - Principle 1: businesses should support and respect the protection of internationally proclaimed human rights; and
    - Principle 2: make sure that they are not complicit in human rights abuses.

- Labour

  - Principle 3: businesses should uphold the freedom of association and the effective recognition of the right to collective bargaining;

  - Principle 4: the elimination of all forms of forced and compulsory labour;

  - Principle 5: the effective abolition of child labour; and

  - Principle 6: the elimination of discrimination in respect of employment and occupation.

- Environment

  - Principle 7: businesses should support a precautionary approach to environmental challenges;

  - Principle 8: undertake initiatives to promote greater environmental responsibility; and

  - Principle 9: encourage the development and diffusion of environmentally friendly technologies.

- Anti-corruption

  - Principle 10: businesses should work against corruption in all its forms, including extortion and bribery.

Since its inception, the Global Compact has been influential in the development of corporate sustainability strategies across many organizations. To support this progress, in 2020, the UN announced a set of benchmarks that can help organizations set ambitious goals across all aspects of the Compact. These benchmarks are:

- Gender balance across all levels of management.

- Zero discharge of pollutants and hazardous chemicals.

- Net-positive water impact in water-stressed basins.

- Zero waste to landfill and incineration.

- 100% resource recovery, with all materials and products recovered and recycled or re-used at end of life.

- Greenhouse gas emissions reduction in line with a 1.5°C pathway.

- Zero incidences of bribery.

SOURCE UN (2020)

Sustainability in the procurement cycle

Procurement's contribution to sustainability can be substantial because it has the potential to influence the entire supply base. The more progressive organizations have realized that procurement decisions have a 'multiplier effect' that trickles through the entire supply base and has the potential to achieve economic, environmental and social change more quickly than almost any other single activity within an organization.

The term *sustainable procurement* refers to the management systems and practices that allow organizations to meet their needs for goods and services, taking a whole life cycle approach across the three dimensions of the 3BL. The term *green procurement* is often used for the environmental aspects of procurement, while *ethical procurement* or *ethical sourcing* relate to the social dimension.

Sustainability should be an integral part of the strategic procurement cycle (Figure 10.2) introduced in Chapter 1. At every stage of the cycle, from defining the vision through to continuous improvement, sustainability criteria should be embedded. Below we describe the main sustainability considerations at each stage of the cycle.

1 Articulate procurement's sustainability vision, mission and goals

Procurement's sustainability vision, mission and goals should align with the organization's sustainability ambitions, but this should not just be a top-down process. Procurement practitioners at all levels should actively seek to engage, inform and influence their organization's approach to sustainability.

In the boardroom, procurement leaders represent the entire supply base and should be responsible for communicating to their colleagues the potential sustainability implications of their decisions. Since for many organizations the most significant sustainability issues lie in the supply chain, it is essential that business leaders recognize the opportunities for and challenges to sustainability across multiple supply chain tiers.

Procurement leaders also need to define their own sustainability vision, goals and objectives. These should take into consideration issues such as supplier engagement, performance measurement, communications, talent management, risk management, technology and innovation.

FIGURE 10.2   Key sustainability questions in the strategic procurement cycle

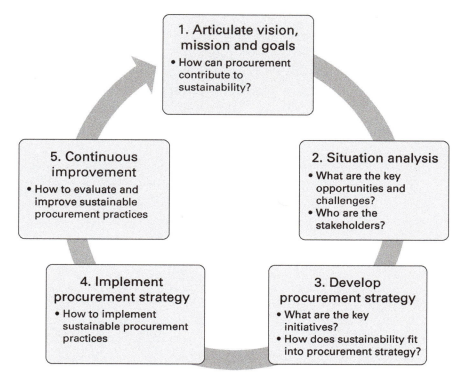

2 *Situation analysis*

As discussed in Chapter 1, a clear understanding of the context in which the organization operates is essential to developing a strategy that is fit for purpose. If procurement professionals are to influence their organization's approach to sustainability, they need to be prepared. They need to understand the impact of their supply chain on different aspects of sustainability and the levers they have at their disposal to improve performance and mitigate risks.

Standard business tools such as market analysis, SWOT and stakeholder analysis can help formulate a sustainable procurement strategy. Having a stakeholder map can help to understand how the different stakeholders can help or hinder our sustainability efforts and to formulate the tactics required to gain their support. Failing to recognize the needs of various stakeholders can undermine sustainability performance and damage the reputation of an organization.

Procurement has some prominent stakeholders, such as suppliers at multiple tiers, internal and external customers. However, sustainability considerations should go beyond the supply chain and include governments, non-governmental organizations (NGOs), auditors and society at large. These stakeholders are critical to achieving sustainability goals and can be either barriers or enablers, depending on how we decide to engage with them. For instance, NGOs, if engaged in the right way, can become trusted allies in supporting the sustainability journey.

Understanding sustainability issues requires tools such as carbon footprinting, life cycle assessment (LCA), through-life costing and risk assessment techniques, which are likely to be relevant at this stage. Some of these tools will be discussed in more detail later in this chapter.

3 Develop a sustainable procurement strategy

Having a clear sustainability vision and goals (stage 1) and a good understanding of the priorities and the context in which the organization operates (stage 2) allows the identification of the strategic alternatives for procurement and the charting of an action plan.

As with any strategic endeavour, it is necessary to define the priorities, taking a long-term view of what is expected with regard to sustainability and how it fits with the rest of the procurement strategy. This long-term vision allows us to create a strategic plan describing the key initiatives to be pursued. Alongside the strategic plan, it is necessary to develop a more specific blueprint that spells out the goals, performance measures, critical success factors and key enablers, as well as the skills and resources required to deliver the sustainability initiatives. A good example of an organization that developed and delivered a sustainability strategy is Google, which has been working on a number of initiatives, both social and environmental (see case study).

4 Implement a sustainable procurement strategy

Implementing a sustainable procurement strategy involves incorporating it into day-to-day procurement operations; from the definition of specifications, through to the selection, negotiation, monitoring and evaluation of suppliers of goods and services.

Procurement involvement in the early stages of new product design and development has long been discussed as an opportunity to influence performance. This early involvement is particularly crucial for sustainability, as procurement expertise is required in the selection of sustainable raw materials, production processes and appropriate sources.

Arguably the most significant impact procurement can have on sustainability is in the area of supplier selection and negotiation. However, for this impact to materialize, it is necessary to have a robust supplier selection process that includes sustainability criteria (eg energy and water utilization, GHG emissions and waste management). The weight given to these criteria will, to a large extent, determine the overall impact procurement can have on sustainability across the supply chain.

Organizations also need to make sure they are fair and transparent in the selection and negotiation process, and that they take care of unethical practices such as corruption and bribery. For instance, Walmart has, as part of its standards for suppliers, cover issues such as underage labour, working conditions and dignity of women. Moreover, they have a clear set of guidelines concerning gifts and entertainment offered to Walmart's employees, conflicts of interest, corruption and bribery practices by suppliers (Walmart, 2020).

CASE STUDY
Sustainable supply chains at Google

When we think about Google, we don't often picture a supply chain. However, if we explore the myriad of digital services they offer, from mail to maps, and the multitude of technological products they sell, including Pixel phones, Chromecast media players and Nest thermostats, we quickly realize that a complex supply chain is behind them. The Google ecosystem, depicted in Figure 10.3, includes over 1,000 suppliers in more than 70 countries. Such a complex global supply chain comes with some undesirable effects, both social and environmental.

FIGURE 10.3 Google supply chain

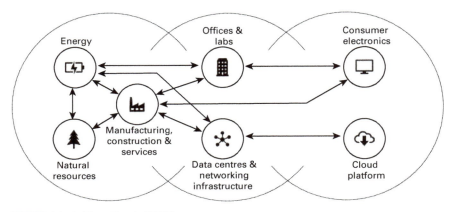

SOURCE Adapted from Google (2018)

To address sustainability concerns in their supply chain, Google is involved in several initiatives around the world. One notable example is their work on responsible sourcing of so-called conflict minerals: tin, tantalum, tungsten and gold. The mining of these minerals has been associated with the financing of armed conflict. Since 2012, Google has moved to source exclusively from smelters and refiners that comply with conflict minerals regulations. In 2018 they achieved 100 per cent compliance across all minerals.

Google has also been actively working with other technology companies and NGOs to eliminate child labour in cobalt mining. The company is also experimenting with blockchain technology to achieve supply chain transparency. In collaboration with Peruvian mining company Minsur, German start-up Minespider and multinationals like Volkswagen and Cisco, Google seeks to use blockchains to provide traceability of minerals throughout the supply chain, from mine to consumer.

Google is also concerned with the environmental impact of its digital services, most notably the use of energy and equipment used in its data centres. Working in partnership with the Ellen MacArthur Foundation, they aim to create a circular economy within the company. This effort has involved changes to the design of their data centres, as well as improved hardware maintenance, involving refurbishment, remanufacturing, redistribution and recycling. The total cost of ownership (TCO) approach used has also saved the company over $1 billion in energy and millions more in equipment. They have even generated income through the resale of 2 million units of equipment to secondary markets.

SOURCES: Ellen MacArthur Foundation (www.ellenmacarthurfoundation.org); Google (2019); Rana and Brandt (2016)

5 Continuous improvement

To maintain and improve sustainability practices across the supply chain, it is necessary to evaluate performance against the goals set in the strategy. This evaluation involves activities within the procurement function as well as those at the suppliers.

The criteria developed to evaluate suppliers at the selection stage can also be used at this stage to assess trends in performance and identify improvement opportunities. While some organizations decide to conduct evaluations by themselves, it is also common to rely on third parties, such as consultants and NGOs, to undertake audits and evaluate suppliers in distant parts of the world. These evaluations, however, should not be used as an excuse to undermine the suppliers but as an opportunity to improve and learn.

Drivers and barriers to sustainable procurement

There is increasing recognition that investments in social and environmental initiatives can bring economic benefits to organizations through efficiency, innovation, improved reputation and risk mitigation. As a result, many public and private organizations have stepped up to the challenge, taking action to work with supply chain partners to improve economic, environmental and social performance.

Below we discuss some of the main reasons companies have cited in support of sustainability initiatives and provide some examples.

Customer value

Companies have started to realize that some customer segments are concerned about the impact of the products they consume on society and the environment. Research has shown that ecologically conscious consumers believe they can help solve environmental problems by voting with their wallet, and other studies show that social responsibility perceptions affect the images of brands and the propensity of consumers to buy specific brands (Ganesan *et al*, 2009). However, there is still debate about how much customers are willing to pay for sustainable products.

Although the jury is still out, many companies are engaging in 'green marketing' as a way to gain or maintain a competitive advantage (Starik and Marcus, 2000). Some have developed premium offerings with strong environmental credentials. An example is Nespresso, a subsidiary of the Swiss food giant Nestlé, which aims to maintain very high environmental and social standards in the sourcing of the materials for their premium coffee capsules, with the ultimate view of delivering sustainable quality.

A company that has taken the notion of sustainability as a source of customer value is Impossible Foods Inc. The company was founded in 2011 with the aim of developing plant-based substitutes for meat products to reduce the environmental burdens associated with meat production (see case study).

Given that procurement and supply chain managers, in general, have a significant impact on sustainability, it is possible to argue that there is great potential for the procurement community to deliver value to the customer and establish a competitive advantage through sustainable practices.

Cost and efficiency

Leaner and more efficient sourcing, production and transportation systems require fewer inputs (eg raw materials, energy, water). By sourcing more efficiently, companies can reduce their environmental impact while simultaneously lowering the costs of inputs and waste disposal.

The economic benefits make efficiency initiatives easy to justify through traditional return on investment (ROI) evaluations. Initiatives such as reducing waste will generally be easier to sell to other stakeholders, both internal and external (Adenso-Díaz and Mena, 2013; Mena *et al*, 2014).

CASE STUDY
Sustainability at Impossible Foods Inc

Karen Mena de Hoyos

Methane is the second most abundant greenhouse gas in the atmosphere after carbon dioxide. It contributes significantly to global warming, and its concentration in the atmosphere has risen by 150 per cent since 1750. To solve the climate crisis, we have to reduce the emission of both carbon dioxide and methane. About 60 per cent of methane comes from anthropogenic sources; one very important source is cattle, through enteric fermentation and manure management. According to the University of Adelaide, cows produce between 70kg and 120kg of methane per year and, worldwide, there are about 1.5 billion cattle. Altogether, this accounts for around 37 per cent of human-related methane emissions. So how has the food industry worked to solve this problem?

Many companies have made efforts to support cleaner ways of meat production that reduces their emissions. For example, at Texas A&M University, they tested the amount of methane produced from different feeding rations given to cattle. This technology is currently being tested by some companies that hope to reduce their carbon footprint. However, very few companies were founded with the goal of reducing worldwide methane emissions. Impossible Foods, founded by Patrick O Brown, hopes to offer a plant-based alternative to help combat this issue.

Impossible Foods Inc hopes to support a cleaner and more sustainable earth by creating 'meat' made from plants. They claim that one burger uses '96% less land, 87% less water, 86% fewer GHG emissions' when compared to their animal-based counterparts. Over the last decade, Impossible Foods' products have skyrocketed in popularity. You can now find many big food chains such as Starbucks and Burger King offering Impossible meat, as well as many supermarkets and smaller restaurants. They have recently made more new products available, such as 'pork' and 'sausage'.

In conclusion, methane is a harmful greenhouse gas emitted by green waste. Cattle is one major contributor to human-related methane emissions. While many meat companies have made efforts to lower the carbon footprint, one has taken a unique approach. Impossible Foods was founded in the hope of a positive environmental impact on our planet. At the moment, both the corporation and its impact on our carbon footprint looks to have a bright future, with, as they claim, a 'healthy balance, of nature, science, and deliciousness'.

SOURCES Impossible Foods (https://impossiblefoods.com/mission/); Mercier (2018); Phys.org (2019)

Risk

Ignoring environmental or social considerations can expose an organization to many risks. Some of the most prominent ones from a procurement perspective are discussed below.

NATURAL RESOURCES AVAILABILITY

Exploitation of natural resources can lead to unsustainable situations, particularly in cases where the rate of consumption exceeds the rate of replenishment or recovery. Fossil fuels are a good example, as the rate of formation is so slow that the resource is considered non-renewable.

Scarcity of natural resources can lead to price volatility and ultimately to unavailability. Given that one of procurement's primary responsibilities is to source the materials required by the organization in an economical and reliable manner, this is a clear and substantial risk that needs to be mitigated. An example of this is IKEA (see Chapter 1), which shows how the organization is actively managing the natural resources required for its operation.

CORPORATE REPUTATION

The perception that an organization is irresponsible with regard to ethical or environmental concerns can severely dent its reputation and affect its brands. The clothing and sportswear industry has been one of the most affected in this respect, with numerous companies such as Primark, Gap and Victoria's Secret suffering reputational risk due to allegations of child labour and slave labour in their supply chains.

This risk can also be seen as an opportunity for a company to develop its reputation as a sustainability leader. For instance, in 2011, Unilever launched the 'sustainable living plan' to halve the environmental footprint of their products and source 100 per cent of their agricultural raw materials sustainably. To do so, they require a high degree of cooperation from their suppliers, including actively measuring and managing the impact of their products across their entire supply chain. This initiative has been a supply-chain-wide effort that has improved Unilever's reputation with suppliers and customers alike.

TABLE 10.1 Drivers and barriers to sustainable procurement

	Drivers/enablers	Barriers
People/organization	• Top management commitment (*) • Culture of sustainability • Increase in education • Corporate headquarters sustainability standards • Greater functional interaction	• Lack of support • Lack of consensus at top level • Internal scepticism
Resources and capabilities	• Alignment with existing resources and capabilities • Attract investment • Access to supplier capabilities	• Lack of resources and capabilities • Suppliers' lack of resources and capabilities
Process/goals	• Collaboration with suppliers (*) • Long-term process perspective • Early supplier engagement in sustainability initiatives • Global sustainability standards • Life cycle thinking • Measurement and reward system • Supply chain visibility	• Misalignment of short- and long-term goals • Lack of sustainability standards • Lack of appropriate regulations • Lack of measures and rewards • Lack of data to evaluate sustainability • Poor supply chain visibility

(continued)

TABLE 10.1 (Continued)

	Drivers/enablers	Barriers
Value	• Customer requirement (*) • Competitive differentiation • Improve relationships with stakeholders • Opportunity to stimulate innovation • Association with improved quality	• Limited customer demand for sustainable products/services (*) • Intangible impact on product/service value
Cost	• Cost savings/improve resource utilization (*) • Avoid environmental taxes • Life cycle costing (LCA) can support long-term decisions	• Initial investments by buyer and supplier (*) • Initiatives can be difficult to evaluate through traditional ROI calculations • Economic uncertainty
Risk	• Compliance with regulation (*) • Reduce pressure from external stakeholders (*) • Influence policy and standards • Reduce reputational damage • Keep up with competitors • Ensure continuity/protect key natural resources	• Additional burden for suppliers • Newness of concept • Scepticism from suppliers • Conflicting strategic objectives with suppliers • Risk of losing suppliers

NOTE (*) Found to be particularly strong drivers/barriers

SOURCES: Carter and Dresner (2001); Giunipero et al (2012); Hoejmose and Adrien-Kirby (2012); Mollenkopf et al (2010); Vachon and Klassen (2008)

REGULATION AND TAXATION

Regional, national and local governments often introduce regulations and taxes to try to protect labour standards and prevent environmental degradation. Research has shown that legislation is an important driver for ecological responsiveness as firms try to prevent fines, penalties and legal costs (Bansal and Roth, 2000). Research has shown that legislation is the sustainability-related issue that has the strongest impact on businesses and that complying with legislation is one of the main motivations for environmental initiatives (Berns *et al*, 2009). Furthermore, proactive organizations can avoid additional expenses by keeping ahead of legislation and even having an opportunity to shape future legislation.

Some regulations are generic, such as health and safety acts that outline the general duties employers have towards employees and members of the public. Others are industry-specific, such as the End of Life Vehicles (ELV) Directive for the automotive industry, and the Waste Electrical and Electronic Equipment (WEEE) Directive and Regulations for the electrical and electronic sector. Taxation and subsidies have also been used to influence environmental practices, such as landfill and carbon taxes.

Despite compelling arguments for action and the efforts of many organizations, sustainable procurement is still in its infancy. A survey by McKinsey (Bonini and Bové, 2014) showed that less than half of their respondents considered sustainability a top priority for the business. Table 10.1 summarizes the main drivers and barriers to sustainable procurement.

Approaches for sustainable procurement

Several tools and techniques are available to tackle sustainability challenges in procurement. Here we have classified these approaches into three main categories: supply chain design, supply chain governance, and mapping and measurement tools. Each of these is discussed below.

Supply chain design (and redesign)

Supply chain design involves critical decisions such as how and where to produce products, how to store and transport them, how many suppliers to have and how to engage with them (Danloup *et al*, 2015). These kinds of decisions can have a very substantial impact on sustainability.

Traditionally supply chains have been seen as linear processes, converting raw materials into finished products. However, sustainability pressures have instigated a different perspective, which promotes a circular, or closed-loop, view of supply chains, in which materials are taken from the ground and returned to the ground or used in some other productive way. Below we describe two approaches using this circular perspective: industrial ecology and Cradle-to-Cradle.

Circular economy and *industrial ecology* are two concepts introduced in the late 1980s that take a systems perspective and propose that supply chains could act as an ecosystem, where the waste of one organization can be used as a resource by another organization. These symbiotic relationships between organizations in the chain not only reduce the requirements for virgin raw materials but also help reduce costs, waste and emissions. This requires a complete redesign of the supply chain and the procurement practices involved.

The most cited example of industrial ecology in practice is the Kalundborg network, operating in the Danish city of the same name. Kalundborg Symbiosis is a public and private partnership in which waste products from industrial production are bought and sold in a closed loop. The network involves several organizations, including a Statoil refinery, the Asnæs power station, Novo Nordisk and the Kalundborg Municipality, which trade products such as steam, heat, slurry, dust and gas that can be physically transported from one organization to another.

It is claimed that, on an annual basis, Kalundborg Symbiosis has reduced CO_2 emissions by 240,000 tons, saved 3 million cubic metres of water through recycling and reuse, converted 30,000 tons of straw to 5.4 million litres of ethanol, and recycled 150,000 tons of gypsum, replacing the import of natural gypsum (Kalundborg Symbiosis, 2017). However, despite its impressive results, Kalundborg appears to be a unique system with few other comprehensive examples of industrial ecology.

In a similar vein, but on a smaller scale, Braungart and McDonough (2008) proposed the concept of *Cradle-to-Cradle (C2C)* as a design approach inspired in biological systems. A central principle of C2C is 'waste = food', suggesting that products be designed so that the 'waste' they generate can be used as inputs (or 'food') for other products and services.

Cradle-to-Cradle requires that all ingredients used and produced across the supply chain be either biological materials, which can be decomposed organically, or technical materials, which are non-toxic materials that have no negative environmental impact. Technical materials can be used in closed-loop cycles without losing their quality or integrity. Figure 10.4 summarizes the concept of Cradle-to-Cradle.

A company that has embraced the principles of the circular economy is Nike. Under the banner of *Space Hippie*, Nike has developed a new generation of shoes that use waste materials from other processes as their main inputs and reduce energy usage and carbon emissions in the process (see case study).

FIGURE 10.4   A schematic view of Cradle-to-Cradle

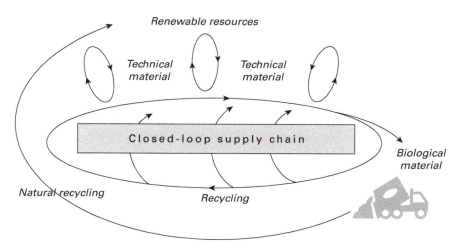

Supply chain governance

Sustainability involves members of the supply chain working together in aspects such as joint environmental goal-setting, shared environmental planning, and cooperation to reduce resource utilization, pollution or other environmental impacts.

A key decision in sustainable procurement is the decision on how the organization will work with its suppliers to tackle sustainability issues. Two main options are available (Winstanley *et al*, 2002):

- *Engagement*: this involves setting standards (eg code of conduct) and compliance procedures for suppliers, and setting longer-term aims to improve standards through collaboration.

- *Disengagement*: this also involves setting clear standards for suppliers, coupled with a means of assessing compliance with those standards (eg audits). Failure to meet standards can lead to disengagement with the supplier.

CASE STUDY
Nike's Space Hippie

Plastic waste has emerged as a significant environmental problem due to its impact on wildlife and human health. It is estimated that every year about 8 million tons of plastic end up in the ocean. To address this problem, the United Nations Environmental Assembly (UNEA) adopted a resolution in 2019, aiming to reduce single-use plastic waste.

Recognizing the waste problem, many companies have engaged in the adoption of a circular economy approach that considers materials utilization at the product design stage and seeks to develop supply chains that recycle materials and minimize waste.

Nike generates yearly revenues of almost $40 billion, and that is a lot of shoes! This scale means that even a small change in the average amount of carbon emitted and waste generated per pair has a significant impact on the environment. The company recognizes this challenge and has committed to a zero-carbon and zero-waste future.

Nike has fostered a circular economy mentality for several years, and in 2020 they introduced an experimental collection called Space Hippie. The collection is inspired by the notion that in a mission to Mars, raw materials would be scarce and resupply missions would be infrequent, so the colonizers would have to use scraps to create any new products. To accomplish this, a team of designers at Nike adopted a radical design approach focused on sustainable practices and relying primarily on recycled materials. In doing so, they produced the shoe with the lowest carbon footprint yet.

The Flyknit yarn used in the construction of the upper is made from 85–90 per cent recycled content from t-shirts, plastic bottles and other scraps. The soles are made of recycled crater foam, which uses about 15 per cent recycled rubber. Finally, they redesigned the packaging, avoiding a secondary box for shipping and using repurposed materials and plant-based paint in the construction of the shoe box.

The Space Hippie collection turned out to be a success, both environmentally and commercially. The entire collection sold out in a matter of days.

SOURCES International Institute for Sustainable Development (https://sdg.iisd.org/); Nike (2019); Nike (2020); Nike 2019 Impact Report; https://www.nike.com/space-hippie

These approaches are not mutually exclusive, and organizations might want to follow a portfolio strategy in which they decide to engage with some suppliers and disengage with others. Each product category is likely to face different sustainability challenges, and it might be necessary to develop specific tactics for each category.

Regardless of which engagement approach a company decides to follow, it will need specific governance mechanisms in place to be able to steer the supply chain in the right direction. These mechanisms can include contracts, standards and codes of conduct. These mechanisms are briefly explained below.

1 CONTRACTS FOR SUSTAINABILITY

Contracts are the most common supply chain governance mechanism. It is possible and increasingly common to include environmental and social clauses in contracts that reflect an organization's sustainability values and strategy. For public organizations, it is also permissible under EU procurement regulations to have special clauses related to sustainability as long as they relate to performance after the contract is awarded and not for supplier selection.

Clauses can include provisions for generic issues such as the development of plans and indicators for sustainability, as well as specific issues such as recycling, use of reusable containers, waste (including packaging), transportation and handling of hazardous substances. Contracts can also refer to other governance mechanisms such as standards and codes of conduct.

2 STANDARDS

Sustainability standards and certifications are sets of norms and principles relating to social, ethical and environmental issues, which organizations adopt voluntarily to showcase their performance in these areas. Standards are produced by international organizations such as the International Organization for Standardization (ISO); national organizations such as the American National Standards Institute (ANSI), the German Institute for Standardization (Deutsches Institut für Normung – DIN) or the British Standards Institution (BSI); and by non-governmental organizations, such as Fairtrade, the Rainforest Alliance, Social Accountability International (SAI) and the Forest Stewardship Council (FSC).

There are hundreds of sustainability standards, and producing a comprehensive list is beyond the purpose of this book. However, to give a sense of the breadth and scope of different standards, we've included a list of some of the most commonly used sustainability standards, which is presented in Table 10.2.

3 CODES OF CONDUCT

Companies will need to develop or adopt a code of conduct that can be used as a guideline for judging supplier sustainability performance. There are several options available, including industry codes (eg ETI base code), professional codes (eg CIPS Code of Conduct – see case study; ISM Principles and Standards of Ethical Supply Management Conduct) or corporate codes (eg Toyota Code of Conduct; Walmart Standards for Suppliers). Furthermore, organizations also have to decide how they intend to evaluate compliance with the codes, and this might involve using a combination of direct involvement and collaboration, as well as audits and assessments by third parties.

TABLE 10.2 Common sustainability standards

Standard	Issuer	Description	Focus		
			Env	Soc	Econ
ISO 14000 family	ISO	A family of certification standards aimed at helping organizations manage environmental issues. It includes ISO 14001, which is a framework for environmental management systems (EMS).	X		
ISO 26000	ISO	A comprehensive standard for social responsibility. It provides guidance rather than requirements, so it cannot be certified.	X	X	X
ISO 20400: 2017	ISO	Guides organizations in integrating sustainability within procurement, as described in ISO 26000.	X	X	
PAS 2050	BSI	Specification for the assessment of the life cycle greenhouse gas emissions of goods and services.	X		
SA8000	SAI	Auditable certification standard that encourages organizations to develop, maintain and apply socially acceptable practices in the workplace.		X	
Fairtrade	Fairtrade	Auditable certification. Its original focus was the guarantee of a minimum price and a social premium for agricultural producers. Recently it has also adopted environmental objectives.	X	X	X
Rainforest Alliance	Rainforest Alliance	A family of certification and verification standards aimed in the areas of conservation, sustainable livelihoods, land-use practices and business practices.	X	X	
FCS	FCS	A set of principles and standards as well as certification and labelling of forest products.		X	

KEY: Env = Environmental; Soc = Social; Econ = Economic

CASE STUDY
CIPS Code of Conduct

Enhance and protect the standing of the profession, by:

- never engaging in conduct, either professional or personal, which would bring the profession or the Chartered Institute of Procurement & Supply into disrepute
- not accepting inducements or gifts (other than any declared gifts of nominal value which have been sanctioned by my employer)
- not allowing offers of hospitality or those with vested interests to influence, or be perceived to influence, my business decisions
- being aware that my behaviour outside my professional life may have an effect on how I am perceived as a professional

Maintain the highest standard of integrity in all business relationships, by:

- rejecting any business practice which might reasonably be deemed improper
- never using my authority or position for my own financial gain
- declaring to my line manager any personal interest that might affect, or be seen by others to affect, my impartiality in decision making
- ensuring that the information I give in the course of my work is accurate and not misleading
- never breaching the confidentiality of information I receive in a professional capacity
- striving for genuine, fair and transparent competition
- being truthful about my skills, experience and qualifications

Promote the eradication of unethical business practices, by:

- fostering awareness of human rights, fraud and corruption issues in all my business relationships
- responsibly managing any business relationships where unethical practices may come to light, and taking appropriate action to report and remedy them
- undertaking due diligence on appropriate supplier relationships in relation to forced labour (modern slavery) and other human rights abuses, fraud and corruption

- continually developing my knowledge of forced labour (modern slavery), human rights, fraud and corruption issues, and applying this in my professional life

Enhance the proficiency and stature of the profession, by:

- continually developing and applying knowledge to increase my personal skills and those of the organization I work for
- fostering the highest standards of professional competence amongst those for whom I am responsible
- optimizing the responsible use of resources which I have influence over for the benefit of my organization

Ensure full compliance with laws and regulations, by:

- adhering to the laws of countries in which I practise, and in countries where there is no relevant law in place I will apply the standards inherent in this Code
- fulfilling agreed contractual obligations
- following CIPS guidance on professional practice

SOURCE https://www.cips.org/who-we-are/governance/cips-code-of-conduct/ This code was approved by the CIPS Global Board of Trustees on 10 September 2013. Used with kind permission of the Chartered Institute of Procurement and Supply (CIPS)

Mapping and measurement tools for sustainable procurement

Tools that help us analyse, understand and measure the impact on sustainability are essential to improve performance. Measuring economic performance has always been at the centre of management activity, and in Chapter 6 we discussed several tools, such as total cost of ownership (TCO) and kaizen costing, which can be used for this purpose (see Google case study). In this section, we will concentrate on discussing some of the main tools that can be used to measure and manage environmental and social aspects.

CARBON FOOTPRINTING

Carbon footprinting involves mapping and measuring the total greenhouse gas emissions (GHG) caused by an organization, event, product or person (Wright *et al*, 2011). Since a carbon footprint considers all the sources, sinks and storage, if we are to measure the carbon footprint of a product, it is necessary to collect data from the entire supply chain. This process requires close collaboration with suppliers and customers.

Once the carbon footprint is understood, it is possible to devise strategies to reduce or compensate for it. Carbon footprints and labels have also been used to show stakeholders about the environmental performance of a product or service. In the UK, the first brand to obtain a carbon label was Walkers crisps in 2007 and the first to retain it in 2009 after reducing its total carbon footprint by 7 per cent (see case study).

LIFE CYCLE ASSESSMENT (LCA)

Life cycle assessment is a tool for assessing all of the environmental impacts associated with every stage of the supply chain. LCAs have a much broader focus than carbon footprints as they compile an inventory of all of the inputs and outputs across the supply chain and then evaluate the potential environmental impacts these can have, such as human toxicity, ozone layer depletion, aquatic acidification, non-renewable energy consumption and mineral extraction.

LCA is a more sophisticated tool than carbon footprints, as it provides a comprehensive evaluation of all of the environmental impacts of a product. However, there are trade-offs. LCAs require much more data, time and expertise to be able to produce a reliable result. These requirements also mean that the evaluation is more expensive. Here companies might be trading off time and money for accuracy and depth of understanding.

There are other tools to measure the environmental impact of products and services, such as water footprinting (Hoekstra *et al*, 2011) and ecological footprinting (Ewing *et al*, 2010), which might be relevant for some organizations. However, carbon footprints and LCAs are most commonly applied.

CASE STUDY

Carbon footprinting and Walkers Crisps

In April 2007, Walkers Crisps started labelling its cheese and onion crisps with a carbon label stating how many grams of CO_2e had been emitted in the production of the product.

The study, conducted in collaboration with the Carbon Trust, revealed that in producing a 37.5 gram bag of crisps, 75 grams of CO_2e were emitted. This included practically all the stages in the supply chain from farming, manufacturing, packaging, distribution, disposal and retailing, but excluded retailing and consumption. Figure 10.5 shows how emissions were distributed across the chain.

FIGURE 10.5   Carbon footprint of a packet of Walkers Crisps

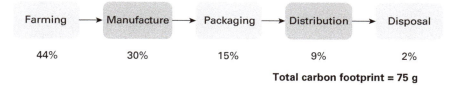

Total carbon footprint = 75 g

The study helped executives at Walkers realize that carbon emissions were mainly driven by raw materials and manufacturing and that energy consumption was a major factor. This meant that the source of energy is a critical decision for this product.

The study also revealed an unexpected opportunity. It showed that since Walkers were buying potatoes by gross weight, farmers were keeping their potatoes in humidified storage to increase the water content. As a result, Walkers had to fry the potatoes for longer to drive out the extra moisture. Both processes consumed unnecessary energy, and by simply changing the buying specification from gross weight to dry weight, Walkers was able to reduce frying time by 10 per cent and remove the motivation for keeping potatoes humidified. This measure helped save energy along with its associated cost and carbon emissions.

Measuring the carbon footprint has helped Walkers reduce its overall carbon footprint by 7 per cent. This includes a 41 per cent reduction in manufacturing gas consumption; a 37 per cent reduction in manufacturing electricity consumption; a 10.5 per cent reduction in the weight of corrugated boxes; a 5 per cent reduction in transport-related emissions; and a 4.5 per cent reduction in emissions associated with packaging.

SOURCE BBC (2007); Carbon Trust (www.carbontrust.com); Economist (2011)

Measuring the social aspects of the triple bottom line is considerably more complicated than the economic and environmental ones. However, the lack of accurate measures should not be an excuse to avoid managing these issues.

There have been some attempts to develop tools to measure social impact. For instance, UNEP (2009) has developed a tool called Social Lifecycle Assessment (S-LCA), which looks after the well-being of different stakeholders such as workers, consumers, local communities and other actors in the supply chain. The S-LCA evaluates several impact categories, including human rights, working conditions, health and safety, cultural heritage, governance and socio-economic repercussions.

While some quantifiable indicators can help us evaluate the impact of procurement decisions on society, the measures lack precision and data collection mechanisms are rarely in place, making it very difficult to conduct reliable assessments. As these tools mature, it will become possible to apply them across the supply chain. However, at this stage, it might be more effective to use other mechanisms such as codes of conduct and audits to ensure the social aspects of sustainability are catered for.

Summary and conclusions

Sustainability challenges can be seen as either risks that need to be mitigated or as opportunities that can create a competitive advantage. For most organizations, it's probably both, as some challenges might require only simple mitigation strategies. In contrast, others, which fit with the organization's values, core competencies and strategies, should be exploited as opportunities to gain competitive advantage.

Pressures to deal with sustainability issues are here to stay, and procurement professionals need to be prepared. We need to understand the impact of their decisions on sustainability and be aware of what needs to be done to improve performance. Given the impact that procurement can have on suppliers at multiple tiers, this is an excellent opportunity for all procurement professionals to take the lead and make a positive contribution to their organization, to the entire supply chain and society at large.

References

Adenso-Díaz, B and Mena, C (2013) Food industry waste management, *Sustainable Food Processing*, ed B K Tiwari, T Norton and N M Holden, pp 435–62, John Wiley & Sons, Chichester

Bansal, P and Roth, K (2000) Why companies go green: a model of ecological responsiveness, *Academy of Management Journal*, **43** (4), pp 717–36

BBC (2007) What's the carbon footprint of a potato? http://news.bbc.co.uk/1/hi/magazine/7002450.stm (archived at https://perma.cc/3RVF-KP8Q)

Berns, M et al (2009) The business of sustainability, *MIT Sloan Management Review*, **51** (1), pp 20–6

Bonini, S and Bové, A-T (2014) Sustainability's strategic worth: McKinsey Global Survey results, 1 July, https://www.mckinsey.com/business-functions/sustainability/our-insights/sustainabilitys-strategic-worth-mckinsey-global-survey-results (archived at https://perma.cc/3MTN-YURH)

Braungart, M and McDonough, W (2008) *Cradle to Cradle: Re-making the way we make things*, Jonathan Cape, London

Carter, C and Dresner, M (2001) Purchasing's role in environmental management: cross-functional development of grounded theory, *Journal of Supply Chain Management*, **37** (3), pp 12–27

CIPS (2017) Code of Conduct, Chartered Institute of Procurement and Supply, https://www.cips.org/en/aboutcips/cips-code-of-conduct/ (archived at https://perma.cc/MU6P-PJ3V)

Danloup, N, Mirzabeiki, V, Allaoui, H, Goncalves, G, Julien, D and Mena, C (2015) Reducing transportation greenhouse gas emissions with collaborative distribution: a case study, *Management Research Review,* **38** (10), pp 1049–67

Economist (2011) Following the footprints, 4 June, http://www.economist.com/node/18750670 (archived at https://perma.cc/WCT9-3H5R)

Ewing, B et al (2010) *Calculation Methodology for the National Footprint Accounts, 2010 Edition*, Global Footprint Network, Oakland, CA

Ganesan, S et al (2009) Supply management and retailer performance, emerging trends, issues, and implications for research and practice, *Journal of Retailing*, **85** (10), pp 84–94

Giunipero, L C, Hooker, R E and Denslow, D (2012) Purchasing and supply management sustainability: drivers and barriers, *Journal of Purchasing and Supply Management*, **18** (4), pp 258–69

Google (2018) Responsible Supply Chain Report 2018, https://www.gstatic.com/gumdrop/sustainability/google-2018-rsc-report.pdf (archived at https://perma.cc/E4XE-MLP6)

Google (2019) Responsible Supply Chain Report 2019, https://www.gstatic.com/gumdrop/sustainability/google-2019-rsc-report.pdf (archived at https://perma.cc/KF55-K4E4)

Hoejmose, S U and Adrien-Kirby, A J (2012) Socially and environmentally responsible procurement: a literature review and future research agenda of a managerial issue in the 21st century, *Journal of Purchasing and Supply Management*, **18** (4) pp 232–42

Hoekstra, A Y *et al* (2011) *The Water Footprint Assessment Manual: Setting the global standard*, Earthscan, London

Kalundborg Symbiosis (2017) A circular ecosystem of economy, http://www.symbiosis.dk/en/ (archived at https://perma.cc/9AEA-GF96)

Lamming, R and Hampson, J (1996) The environment as a supply chain management issue, *British Journal of Management*, **7** (s1), pp S45–S62

Mena, C *et al* (2014) Causes of waste across multi-tier supply networks: cases in the UK food sector, *International Journal of Production Economics*, **152**, pp 144–58

Mercier, S (2018) How improved practices could reduce livestock's greenhouse gas footprint, AgWeb, 11 January, https://www.agweb.com/opinion/how-improved-practices-could-reduce-livestocks-greenhouse-gas-footprint (archived at https://perma.cc/6F2P-RGA7)

Mollenkopf, D *et al* (2010) Green, lean, and global supply chains, *International Journal of Physical Distribution and Logistics Management*, **14** (1/2), pp 14–41

Nike (2019) Annual Report 2019, https://investors.nike.com/investors/news-events-and-reports/default.aspx (archived at https://perma.cc/QLS5-A3HM)

Nike (2020) Annual Report 2020, https://investors.nike.com/investors/news-events-and-reports/default.aspx (archived at https://perma.cc/QLS5-A3HM)

Phys.org (2019) Study shows potential for reduced methane from cows, 5 July, https://phys.org/news/2019-07-potential-methane-cows.html (archived at https://perma.cc/3XNH-3AHH)

Rana, S and Brandt, K (2016) Circular economy at work in Google data centers, Google, https://static.googleusercontent.com/media/www.google.com/en//green/pdf/data-center-case-study.pdf (archived at https://perma.cc/3XM8-R6WP)

Starik, M and Marcus, A (2000) Introduction to the special research forum on the management of organisations in the natural environment: a field emerging from multiple paths, with many challenges ahead, *Academy of Management Journal*, **43** (4), pp 539–47

UN (1987) Brundtland Commission – Report of the World Commission on Environment and Development: Our Common Future, https://sustainabledevelopment.un.org/content/documents/5987our-common-future.pdf (archived at https://perma.cc/9YDV-YVJL)

UN (2020) UN Global Compact defines new level of ambition for corporate sustainability, 9 June, https://www.unglobalcompact.org/news/4575-06-09-2020 (archived at https://perma.cc/ZP97-CTBQ)

UNEP (2009) Guidelines for Social Life Cycle Assessment of Products, United Nations Environment Programme, ISBN: 978-92-807-3021-0

Vachon, S and Klassen, R D (2008) Environmental management and manufacturing performance: the role of collaboration in the supply chain, *International Journal of Production Economics*, **111** (2), pp 299–315

Walmart (2020) Responsible sourcing, https://corporate.walmart.com/responsible-sourcing (archived at https://perma.cc/XLL3-YYHJ)

Winstanley, D, Clark, J and Leeson, H (2002) Approaches to child labour in the supply chain, *Business Ethics: A European Review*, **11** (3), pp 210–23

Wright, L, Kemp, S, Williams, I (2011) 'Carbon footprinting': towards a universally accepted definition, *Carbon Management*, **2** (1), pp 61–72

11

The future of procurement

REMKO VAN HOEK

The future of procurement is bright and exciting. On the back of four decades of procurement development and industry progress, professionals in procurement are at an exciting crossroads where a path forward can be charted. In this chapter we will lay out what that path might look like and share examples of companies that are already on it.

By the end of this chapter you should have a clear sense of key focus areas in the future of procurement. And you will have a good feel for how dynamic the path to the future will be and that this path will likely continue to evolve and change as leaders in the field push the boundaries of practice. If nothing else, we hope you will get a sense for how exciting and professionally rewarding working in the procurement field can be, even if just for a short period of time.

This chapter is heavily based upon the recent publication in the anniversary issue of the *Journal of Purchasing and Supply Management*, in which we collaborated with executives to detail key topics for the future of procurement (van Hoek *et al*, 2020).

The direction of progress in procurement

SCM World, a Gartner company, conducted a global survey involving close to 300 respondents on changes in the role of procurement between now and 2025 (see Figure 11.1) When contrasting the dark bars, representing today's role, with the lighter bars representing the anticipated role of procurement in 2025, several interesting patterns emerge:

1 A move from strategic sourcing to SRM. When considering that the focus on sourcing as much external spend as possible is expected to become a minor focus area, this implies that most companies anticipate reaching maturity in strategic sourcing to the degree that they will have the majority of external spend sourced and under contract. As a result, the focus of the procurement team can move more towards SRM and the management of those relationships.

2 A move beyond basic sourcing strategies. While many sourcing strategies may be put in place, these obviously need to be updated as business needs and supplier markets evolve; you are never done with strategic sourcing. But what the top bar in Figure 11.1 implies is that basic and simple sourcing strategies (eg, the left-hand side of the sourcing gemstone in Chapter 3), focused on a growing scale to create leverage in negotiating costs, will be on the decline but costs will still be important.

3 Risk management and supplier performance management are here to stay; they were, are and will be important.

4 Supply availability for customer satisfaction, and agile processes and speed of support are customer- and market-facing focuses that are set to become more important. This implies that procurement is more capable in its business partnering and impacting/supporting market effectiveness, and that it is able to link more directly to customers and markets; procurement is becoming a driver of customer value, not just an upstream function focused on suppliers and far removed from the customer.

5 In that process, new focus areas emerge as being directly on procurement's plate – innovation and corporate social responsibility in particular. Clearly, these represent key customer-value drivers and they cement procurement's role in 'winning in the market' as well as

'helping make the world a better place', only making procurement more exciting as a function!

6 Two aspects possibly missing from this image of the future are the role of talent in building the future and the enabling role of technology in that process. Arguably, the talent of the future is what stands between the vision for the future and the realization of that vision.

In the following sections, we will cover supplier-enabled innovation, corporate social responsibility, technology and talent as keys to the path to 2025 and beyond.

Supplier-enabled innovation (SEI): not for the weak at heart

Supplier relationship management is very much the price of entry to supplier-enabled innovation. A lot of companies fall into the pitfall of going straight to innovation. They invite suppliers to an event and

FIGURE 11.1 Roles of procurement

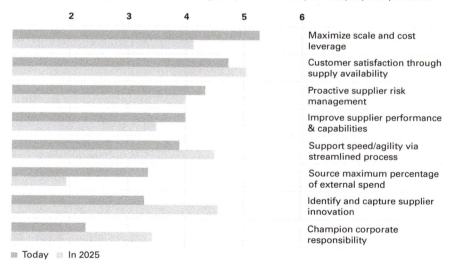

What are the most important roles of sourcing and procurement in your company today? In 2025?

- Maximize scale and cost leverage
- Customer satisfaction through supply availability
- Proactive supplier risk management
- Improve supplier performance & capabilities
- Support speed/agility via streamlined process
- Source maximum percentage of external spend
- Identify and capture supplier innovation
- Champion corporate responsibility

■ Today ▨ In 2025

Weighted average rating (1-8), n=294

SOURCE Gartner SCM World Future of Supply Chain Survey 2018

ask them to share. This is a very risky proposition. If the procurement team for decades has focused on sourcing and has not been a constant factor in the supplier relationship after the contracting stage, suppliers will likely mistrust the effort. Is this another way to ask for a discount? Innovation requires a lot of joint work, just as in contract implementation and continuous improvement, but procurement has traditionally not engaged in this – why would they now and do so well? Long story short, procurement teams are advised to develop SRM capability first, as a pathway to innovation.

Practical ways to get started with SRM include:

1 **Don't be surprised if there is a large push back from your own team**
   The pitfalls from Figure 11.2 list some of the things often said by buyers concerned about moving into SRM. And parts of these concerns are right. But with tooling, a playbook, new technology and a realistic approach, SRM can really grow procurement's contribution and involvement in business success.

2 **Don't go too far too soon, you are likely starting from behind**
   As mentioned, suppliers may not recognize procurement in the relationship and SRM represents a whole new process and playbook, so ensure the necessary homework is done. It is easy to fall short in relationships.

3 **Develop your playbook**
   There are likely to be elements of SRM practice already around the company; collecting these is a good start. Developing a playbook for buyers, the business and suppliers is even better. It helps make sure we are all set to really deliver. While technology can really help here, starting with simple supplier segmentation schemes and dashboards can already represent a step up.

4 **Find your levers with the business and suppliers**
   The business likely sees the suppliers as 'their suppliers', and they are. In particular, if procurement has been largely absent from the relationship it needs to earn its way in. With the business, that may be offering to get a good continuous improvement process going.

With the suppliers, it may be to establish a structured bilateral relationship about the collaboration.

5 **Start realistically and scale with results, but don't get ahead of yourself**
Couple new tools, roles and process with the reality that managing supplier relationships is a lot of work that is ongoing and hands-on, and it becomes obvious that starting realistically is key. A pilot universe of suppliers and stakeholders can be a very wise approach to reduce the risk of non-delivery. As results are generated and experience grows, it is likely that requests for inclusion of more relationships will come in. This is a good way to scale, driven by business pull.

6 **While a dedicated team and capability may be needed, eventually this becomes part of the new normal**
The playbook development, new process design, technology upgrade and the SRM pilot may all be done by a dedicated team. At the initial stages the programme will benefit from some resources, but once it is fully up to speed some of the tools and work will become everybody's business. It will become part of the new normal and the new way of adding value and serving not just the business, but now also suppliers.

P&G was one of the first companies to recognize that a lot of the R&D that goes into its products happens in the supply chain, outside of its own lab. And with C-suite support, procurement embarked on a process that changed procurement practice to begin to target supplier-enabled innovation in a number of ways:

1 **Supplier awards are a good starting point to say thank you and change the conversation**
While they may appear trivial, creating an opportunity to say thank you via supplier awards can go a long way to beginning to change the conversation with suppliers. And it certainly boosts supplier commitment and business engagement.

2 Asking a supplier how we are as a customer is very powerful
Suppliers know your business well and often they know more about their business with your company than procurement does. CRM tools are better than SRM tools traditionally and there are a lot more account managers than there are buyers. P&G found that asking suppliers for feedback and suggestions went a long way. Suppliers are typically happy to share improvement suggestions and don't often have a mechanism to do so. Asking this question started getting P&G into the conversations they wanted to have.

3 Break the old negotiations rule and be willing to share what you don't know
P&G had to publish where it was hoping for supplier suggestions and this was uncomfortable at first. Old-school negotiations use information asymmetry and focus on creating leverage and the upper hand, not revealing weakness and lack of expertise.

4 Create navigators that can really steward supplier suggestions; this is not a suggestion box
Just inviting suggestions is like hanging a suggestion box on the wall. What P&G found, right after starting to ask suppliers for feedback, is that suppliers often don't know where to go with their suggestions and are often not heard. P&G procurement seized that opportunity to get into innovation by creating navigator roles. These professionals would navigate P&G's complex organization for the suppliers and steward the discussion suppliers wanted to have with the business. It earned procurement a lot of credit with suppliers and the business appreciated the great suggestions that came to them with the help of procurement.

Supplier-enabled innovation (SEI) is a focus on involving suppliers in the creation of new product/service propositions for the buying firm, to drive revenue growth and new customer value. It marks the completion of the journey of procurement into the in-depth ongoing engagement of supplier relationships, and from ensuring supplies from upstream in the supply chain to driving new business in the market. There are at least three types of models for SEI. The case study from Electrolux illustrates the approach of working with existing suppliers to jointly develop new products and accelerate the new product development road map of the company. This approach is similar to that taken by P&G and other consumer products companies, including Unilever.

Vattenfall, the European energy company, takes more of an innovation-scouting approach. Within the procurement function it has created a small dedicated team that will scout the supplier universe for possible technology solutions that can help solve the company's technology challenges or could lead to new market propositions. For example, it formed a joint venture with a company that makes robots for underground use to lay cables.

Vodafone uses more of an accelerator approach. It will invest in promising companies and technologies that it can potentially bring into the market or that with its support can ramp up growth and market potential.

CASE STUDY

Electrolux's supplier-enabled innovation programme

Electrolux is a manufacturer of domestic appliances such as dishwashers and vacuum cleaners. The company has developed a programme to boost innovation based upon joint innovation efforts with suppliers. The programme was started based upon the simple realization that suppliers spend more money on R&D than Electrolux can on its own. The programme contains several key elements:

- Electrolux has openly published to suppliers the areas and technologies where it is seeking input. This helps ensure the relevance of suggestions as well as a true commitment to considering suggestions.

- The company scouts and reviews supplier suggestions and has a filtering process for this in which the CEO participates in the final stages of the filtering.

- This process includes supplier presentations and guaranteed feedback from Electrolux to the suppliers. This helps reduce the risk of suppliers feeling that they are not considered and that their ideas go into a black hole or a suggestion box.

- For ideas that are selected, joint innovation teams are formed and an exclusive relationship is formed with the supplier. In this relationship Electrolux commits exclusively to the supplier in return for having exclusive access.

The company has received 2,000 suggestions in the first two to three years of operating the programme. Of these, 350 were presented for consideration, and about 100 went into development. One of the example outcomes is the dishwasher with a bottom drawer on hinges that raises up to make it easier to load and unload dishes. This suggestion came from a supplier in the furniture industry and led to a 'new to the world' feature in dishwashers.

There is a road map towards successful SEI, as Figure 11.2 shows.

A key point to the road map is that there are internal preparations that companies need to go through before calling a supplier meeting or innovation summit. These include the need to establish internal alignment around the potential and opportunity of SEI. Without the

FIGURE 11.2 Road map towards SEI readiness

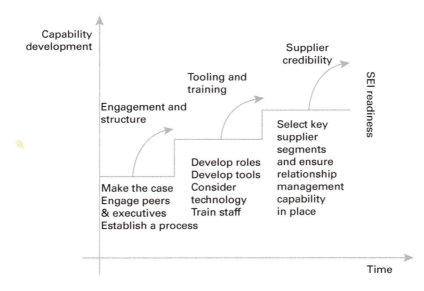

engagement of peer functions such as R&D and product development, the effort might fail. Equally so, it is crucial that C-level executives are willing to engage, participate in supplier meetings and commit R&D investment towards joint innovation opportunities.

The establishment of a process for SEI, likely as an extension of the SRM process, helps to structure efforts, and ensures that there is clear follow-through on supplier suggestions and active management of the opportunity pipeline. It will help grow confidence with suppliers in the programme and may raise their willingness to share innovation suggestions with the company and not its competitors.

The procurement team supporting and facilitating the process is likely to have to develop some additional tools, and potentially technology, and go through some training to enhance its skill set and capability. Table 11.1 shows the changes in role, focus and contribution for procurement that SEI implies. Whereas in strategic sourcing the focus is on optimizing existing spend, SEI turns attention to potential future spend. Whereas in sourcing procurement optimizes spend for savings and efficiency, in SEI it moves towards a focus on new revenue opportunities and accelerating time to market for innovations by collaborating with suppliers. As a result, supplier interactions change. Procurement's role as a gatekeeper to the business becomes one of navigating the supplier through the organization, stewarding innovative suggestions and openly sharing the company's innovation needs and 'unknowns', where suggestions are welcome. The procurement plan becomes less focused on managing spend and contracting through strategic sourcing, and more on how to accelerate following the company's innovation road map.

None of these steps will work without the company having established credibility with suppliers, through its SRM efforts, as a meaningful and trustworthy customer of choice. Without that, the basis for a discussion about joint innovation may not be there; it may not be clear without a supplier segmentation which suppliers are candidates to include in the programme, and the relationship governance and management may not be in place to build upon.

TABLE 11.1 Changes in procurement

Traditional procurement		SEI capable procurement
Existing spend	Spend focus	Future spend
Savings	KPIs	Revenue/time to market
What we want to tell you (poker face)	Supplier interactions	What we don't know (sharing weaknesses)
Gatekeeper	Supplier handling	Navigator
Conclusion	Supplier contract	Beginning
Seeing the past and the current	System enablement	Finding the future
Sourcing waves	Procurement plan	Innovation road map

Industry 4.0: the future of work in procurement

The continued evolution of technology will have a tremendous impact on procurement. Old roles will be automated, perhaps even performed by robots, and new tools will be added to procurement professionals' arsenal. For example, having good data about spend and supplier markets is key to establishing sourcing strategies. Sharing data with stakeholders is often seen by stakeholders as valuable. Machine learning and big data will boost intelligence and can supercharge sourcing strategy development.

Equally so, blockchain changes information rules. While traditional negotiation strategies use information asymmetry to the advantage of the buyer, the public nature of agreements and transactions on blockchain means more complete information is openly available. As a result, the negotiation can focus on what the usage of this information suggests are true solutions and paths forward in business.

Automation and robotization can be a huge blessing. For example, in the requisition-to-pay (R2P) process, there tends to be pressure on process reliability, the cost of the process and the slowness of it. The R2P team performs a critical role in the company, but not one that is always appreciated to its fullest and one where small things can easily go wrong. It may be for its highly administrative process rigour and vulnerability to glitches that a lot of robotization pilots and investments in procurement are in this domain. If it can free up team members to focus more on analysis and reporting while reducing costs and boosting reliability, speed and accuracy, why not?

Social media will drive more real-time market information. Rather than static market intelligence reports, buyers will be able to have a real-time feed to complement this. Rather than a quarterly supplier scorecard review, real-time issues will not have to wait until the next supplier business review.

In summary, Industry 4.0 is not so much about automating jobs away but rather about augmenting jobs to enable productivity and new levels of service.

Talent of the future: why consider a role in procurement?

The past: talent dumping ground?

In the past, when procurement was less about relationships, strategic sourcing and impacting critical priorities such as CSR and innovation, procurement talent was thought of differently than it is today. Procurement did not have the best image in the internal talent market of many companies, or at business schools and universities as a possible function of choice. Some executives used to think of procurement as the place you sent staff away to so that you never saw them again. In the past the performance bar was perhaps lower and simpler; procurement was more operational, had a narrower scope and did not manage critical relationships and contributions to strategic priorities. The skill set was more administrative and negotiations-focused, and less business-centric.

The rise of the strategic sourcing superhero

In moving into the strategic sourcing domain, the increased return (potential) on procurement is typically used to justify greater investment in procurement leaders and teams. The requirements for talent in strategic sourcing include the need to align internally, engage business leaders, work in cross-functional teams, think strategically and manage complex tender processes from specification to implementation.

This stage drives more impactful and strategic thinking into the function and sets the function up not just to do better but also begin to do different – the stage that more advanced organizations are currently in.

New DNA

With a procurement agenda expanding into areas such as CSR, managing supplier relationships and accelerating innovation while reducing risk, different behaviours and skills are required of procurement talent. Critical skills include openness to learn from suppliers, ability to creatively develop (alternative) solutions for business problems, ability to sell and represent, as an ambassador, the enterprise in the supply base, ability to envision ways to competitively differentiate the company, and connect supply-base market intelligence to customer opportunities and strategic goals, relationship and engagement skills.

These skills mirror those wanted in other functions such as marketing and strategy, and mirror common definitions of (future) general managers. This places procurement squarely in the internal talent market. With it comes the opportunity to stop recruiting mostly from within the procurement discipline and actually bring in talent from outside the function, as well as let talent move out of procurement (back) into the business. With that, procurement becomes as much a possible part of the career paths of future leaders as many other functions, such as sales, strategy and finance.

Put simply, none of what is discussed in this chapter will be accomplished without talent. And with the bright future that we describe, procurement is going to have to somewhat reinvent itself from a talent perspective. While in the past expertise in procurement might have been the objective, increasingly it is a price of entry. Stakeholders do not want to learn about procurement: that is your job. What they would like to see is how you can help resolve business challenges and use procurement to make the business better. With that comes a range of characteristics that mirror those of future general managers (GMs). In fact, if you compare job postings for procurement executives today, they are beginning to look surprisingly similar to those for COOs and GMs. To succeed in climbing the ladder of procurement progress requires at least:

- strong communication skills;
- an ability to quickly understand business issues and suggest approaches for tackling them;
- strategic thinking and hands-on delivery of real results;
- relationship skills, with both internal and external stakeholders;
- project management and change management skills;
- ability to lead 'so others will follow';
- ability to manage across borders and cultures;
- pride in serving the business without seeking to take credit for stakeholder results.

It is for all of the above that executives are increasingly engaging with the business schools that are helping develop this talent. To get early access, to inspire talent and to contribute to its development.

While commonly misperceived as less 'sexy' than finance, strategy or marketing, procurement is very interesting for talent of the future to consider, even if just for a temporary assignment. Here are six reasons why:

1 Procurement doesn't only impact a large or very large part of the P&L, it is also exposed to almost all business areas. Think about it: which function does not buy externally and what part of the company does procurement not have licence to engage with? As a result, procurement professionals can get very broad exposure to all parts of the company.

2 Procurement is a critical enabler of many modern business ambitions, including sustainability and diversity. Because of the role that the supplier universe can play in reducing the environmental impact of the supply chain, often far larger than your own company individually,

procurement can be a key lever to a company's sustainability ambitions. Equally so, by allocating spend to diverse suppliers, procurement can contribute massively to diversity objectives.

3 Procurement drives demonstrable, visible ROI to executive decision makers. Through strategic sourcing or the management of key supplier relationships, procurement can drive project returns that are quantifiable and demonstrable to the executives directing the projects. Obviously, these are great to have on any professional résumé.

4 Procurement offers a dynamic project environment while linking to business continuity in demonstrable ways. With procurement impacting all areas of spend across the company, it offers a dynamic and diverse environment where a lot is achieved via projects. Essentially, every day in procurement is different.

5 Procurement skills of the future are those of future GMs. The change management, stakeholder management and communication skills required for effective procurement delivery are what many GMs would say makes them effective and CEO material. Hence, even if only working in procurement for a period of time, it can help any professional hone critical skills for the future.

6 Procurement is expanding its contribution to the supply chain, including revenue and innovations. Progressive procurement organizations are able to expand their role in the wider supply chain, impacting global logistics, sustainability and reputation.

Summary and conclusions

Procurement has come a long way since the first *Harvard Business Review* article speaking to its strategic importance (see Foreword by Peter Kraljic); and it has a long way to go! We have only just begun to realize procurement's potential, and most businesses haven't even begun to experience what that may mean for their growth and performance. In this chapter we have introduced a pathway forward, a number of pitfalls to avoid and a set of emerging topics. While the list of emerging topics will grow and change, one thing is clear: it is an exciting time to be in procurement!

Epilogue: procurement should 'shoot like a girl'

Lessons for procurement from a Purple Heart recipient: stand up for the right to serve, make the mission better and earn respect

Major Mary Jennings Hegar's book *Shoot Like a Girl* shares her incredible story about service, standing up to get a fair opportunity to serve and getting recognized for the capability to serve. Major Hegar's lessons hold a lot of relevance for procurement professionals in modern business, making the lessons well worth considering. The story offers a lot of inspiration and encouragement for the talent of the future that will help shape our profession, hopefully into more of what it can be, as a service to the business.

Major Hegar served in the US Air Force as a medivac helicopter pilot, and served three tours in Afghanistan. During one of her missions, she was shot by the Taliban but continued to fly, and when she and her crew had to abandon their helicopter, she helped protect the patients from enemy fire until they, and all of her crew, were rescued.

During her Air Force career, Major Hegar was often discriminated against because of being a woman, and she ended up suing the US Department of Defense to remove the ban on women fighting in combat. Her story is one of incredible determination to serve and of working incredibly hard to earn the opportunity to serve, going against all discrimination and unfair rules. She not only earned the respect of the crews that she served with, but also came top of her class in the academy, was awarded the Purple Heart and the Distinguished Flying Cross with Valor. The motto of her and her crew was: 'these things we do so others may live'.

Among the learnings and issues Major Hegar shares are:

1 Succeeding academically in combination with practical training is a condition *sine qua non*, and Major Hegar studied and studied, trained and trained to be ready when the opportunity to deploy and serve came.

2 There are physical advantages to being a woman in combat; women are often better at targeting in combat, for example.

3 'When my training unit was broken up into a group that had broad ranges of ages, genders, and skills, I knew we'd be a strong team.'

4 Her stellar performance earned her the respect of fellow students, crew and leadership.

5 While women were not allowed to be in combat, they were needed by commanders and they worked around the rule by 'temporarily assigning' women. This, however, meant that women could not train with the other team members or receive benefits from the Department of Veteran Affairs.

Regarding point 1, procurement professionals need to be ready both academically and practically for when the call comes. You cannot just show up at a business meeting and start figuring out what procurement might be able to do or how things work; you need to be ready to serve, and your skills and expertise are assumed. Those are the price of entry. You don't show it off, you use it to contribute.

Still today, procurement professionals are often not invited into all of the discussions in the company that they should. In fact, 'the percentage of external spend impacted' is a commonly used metric; what this means is that procurement is often not involved in spending the company's money with suppliers. It is why procurement professionals should stand up for the opportunity to serve all areas of spend.

And procurement professionals should stand up for a fair chance to serve, not one in which they are set up to fail or are not really on the team. So don't invite procurement in at the end of the process when all decisions are already made. And don't put them on the spot to see if they can make the deal better without having been on the team all along and 'training' with the others. And give credit where this is due.

Procurement should also look towards diverse perspectives – from women, international perspectives, different functional domains, and so on. This can make the solution to business challenges better, grow the talent pool (which is desperately needed) and, with all the change coming, will better position procurement for future talent requirements.

Furthermore, procurement professionals should be proud to serve. While they may be supporting the business and not owning the budget, 'these things they do so the business will sustain and grow'.

Finally, procurement professionals need to be aware of stakeholder politics and procedures, just like Major Hegar had to. But she found a way through in the end, and ended up changing the rules, as a credible spokesperson based upon her track record. In there is an aspiration for procurement and modern business: know the rules and politics of the company but stand up for the opportunity to serve, deliver award-worthy results and challenge the rules based upon track record, so that the rest of the team and the talent of the future may have an even better chance to drive value and to serve and contribute.

During her keynote speech at the CSCMP Edge Conference, Major Hegar complemented her story with leadership tips that are equally relevant for procurement leaders to consider:

1 Don't rely on altruism too much.

2 Be the change.

3 Know your audience and 'what's in it for them'.

4 Use an empathy, not enemy, approach.

5 Hold on to your 'Why'.

'Don't rely on altruism too much' is obviously impacted by all the unfair hurdles Major Hegar faced during her career. It holds relevance for procurement; all too often are we told; 'We will certainly involve you when there is a need'. Well, in my experience, you should not wait for the phone to ring; you should remind stakeholders about their commitment a few weeks in, when they have not called yet.

'Be the change' holds a lot of relevance for procurement leaders. If you would like to unleash the full power of procurement, lead by example and be proud to serve so that you can earn the opportunity to change things for the better. Don't tell your teams what to do and go back to your office. Open doors for your teams, get meetings for them and help them get ready, join the discussion and make it an issue when they do not get a fair chance. That is your privilege as a leader – to be able to be the change.

Knowing your audience and leading with empathy should be stakeholder management 101 for procurement leaders and something leaders can inspire in their teams. There is no need to argue with stakeholders about not being part of the team, or engage in political warfare. Better to be able to articulate how you would like to try to support and serve, and do so in a way that addresses the stakeholders' concerns and issues.

During her presentation Major Hegar displayed great humility; every achievement was coupled with statements about how they weren't meant to say anything about her. This offers another takeaway for procurement leaders: don't show off with your results. Highlight them but don't claim them, let them be the business's success. If you claim them, your stakeholders might have mixed feelings; it is their business, their spend, they collaborated with you during the sourcing process and they will need to be a key party to the implementation. More importantly, you want stakeholders to invite you back. So, don't put distance between you and them; rather, have the business present the results and graciously accept their accolade and gratitude.

And finally, do not get bogged down in politics or results reporting, hold on to your why. Procurement has a lot to offer to help grow the business and make it more meaningful for customers and society. We do this so that others will benefit! Being a buyer is not a life or death role, nor a contribution to national defence, but buyers can learn from, and be inspired by, the service of heroes like Major Hegar.

Reference

Van Hoek, R, Sankaraman, V, Udesen, T, Geurts, T and Palumbo-Miele, D (2020) Where we are heading and the research that can help us get there – executive perspectives on the anniversary of the Journal of Purchasing and Supply Management, *Journal of Purchasing and Supply Management*, **26** (3), June

INDEX

The main index is filed in alphabetical, word-by-word order. Acronyms are filed as presented. Numbers are filed as spelled out, with exception of ISO standards, which are filed in chronological order. Page locators in italics denote information within a figure or table.